From Otters To Badger Baiters

Malcolm J Ingham

The sequel to From Badgers to Nighthawks

Foreword by Rob Taylor QPM

BeulAithris
Publishing

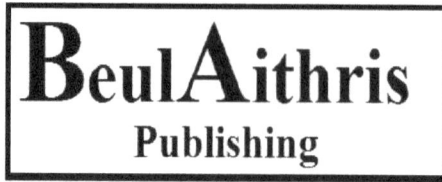

Text © Malcolm J Ingham

'Wildlife Justice' illustration & cover art © Mark Hetherington

ISBN 978-1-917202-01-5

'Wildlife Justice'

Dedication

In memory of my dear friend
John Milne Harrop MBE
A passionate advocate of all things wildlife

And not forgetting my two trail camera checking
companions
Moggy the cat & Nellie the sheepdog

Picture Credits

Back cover photo by kind permission of the Daily Post Wales

Others by Malcolm J Ingham

'Wildlife Justice' cartoon by Mark Hetherington

Contents

Acknowledgments

Firstly, to my wife Ann for her support, advice, and hours of proof reading.

Secondly to John and Sue Harrop for their friendship and allowing me the freedom to roam their land.

And finally, to Rob Taylor QPM for writing the foreword.

Foreword

By Rob Taylor QPM
Wales Rural & Wildlife Police Crime Coordinator

With a passionate lifelong interest for wildlife and with 21 years of police service in North Wales, I was fortunate to be appointed with my dream job as the lead Wildlife and Habitat investigator in 2007, seconded to the Countryside Council for Wales. This organisation would ultimately become Natural Resources Wales as it amalgamated with the Environment Agency and Forestry Commission in Wales broadening its effectiveness. During this time, I was shocked by the scale of wildlife crime in Wales and throughout the UK, whether it was the digging of a badger sett by uncaring and brutal offenders, the destruction of a bat roost or the damage to the habitat of our most precious residents. After being asked to start the first designated Rural Crime Team in the UK in 2013, within North Wales Police, having specialist trained police officers was vital for this new role and I was fortunate to meet a man with not only the passion but the expertise to provide us with that expert knowledge and training that we required.

Mal Ingham having an in depth knowledge of wildlife, their routines and habits was crucial to us by not only understanding the law, but also providing that expert opinion to support our many prosecutions. Mal became that expert who would always give his time, knowledge, and support for free.

He brought priceless years of experience, tied in with a willingness to help our rural team whenever called upon and to this day, many years later, continues to do so. My role changed in 2021 when, as a reappointed police civilian manager, I was handed the responsibility of Wales Wildlife and Rural Coordinator, a newly formed post and first for not only Wales but the UK.

Mal remains to this day my 'go to' expert when addressing wildlife offences involving mammals and their habitats. His outstanding contribution to protect our wildlife cannot be underestimated and I'm honoured to call him a friend and to be able to provide the foreword for this fascinating book.

Preface

As a scruffy kneed kid growing up in the Lancashire market town of Clitheroe nestled deep in the Ribble Valley, I was allowed the freedom to roam and explore the hills, fields, rivers, and woods around my home. The countryside and its wildlife cast a spell over me that sowed the seed of my ambition to become a ranger and work within the realms of wildlife conservation. I eventually achieved my ambition not only to become a ranger but also Head Ranger and Wildlife Officer.

I eventually formed the Wirral Wildlife Rehabilitation Unit which over many years cared for and successfully rehabilitated many species of wildlife gaining an international reputation in the field of wildlife care and rehabilitation.

My work also involved assisting the police and RSPCA in the investigation of wildlife crime taking me into the dark, sinister world of the badger diggers and baiters. My many experiences of working with wildlife gave me the impetus to put pen to paper finally resulting in the publication of my first book *From Badgers to Nighthawks* followed by *The Tales of Old Billy Badger*.

Upon officially retiring from the ranger service and relocating to North Wales I filled my time by utilising trail cameras to monitor and record the secret lives of otters and badgers plus a host of other species and fully expected my work of confronting badger diggers and baiters and investigating their heinous crimes to be a thing of the past. But the police and RSPCA Special Ops Unit had other ideas and were soon once again knocking on my door requesting assistance in their investigations which, needless to say, dragged me from retirement back into the sordid cruel world of these wildlife criminals.

This book contains tales of the trials and tribulations of giving expert prosecution evidence and the intense cross-examination by defence lawyers whilst taking the stand.

The impetus to writing From *Otters to Badger Baiters* came from the many requests for a sequel to my first book *From Badgers to Nighthawks* plus the accumulation of many more new stories relating to my countless investigations and court cases plus of course a plethora of wildlife tales from the badger Nutter clan and their interaction with otters and sheep. From an otter leaping out of the water to nip a badger on the bum to badger cubs climbing onto the back of a ewe as she chills out around the sett contentedly chewing her cud.

Plus, there are also tales of filming for such programmes as BBC Wales Investigates 'The Secret World of Badger Baiters' the ITV Wales programme 'Coast and Country' and Channel 5's 'Badgers: Their Secret World'.

My passion for wildlife is as strong now as it was all those years ago as a scruffy kneed Clitheroe kid clutching to a dream of becoming a wildlife ranger.

1

Muffles & Velvet & The Whistling Fox

"Malcolm! What are we going to do about these damn foxes?" came the totally unexpected and gob smacking question from the grey headed moustached figure, his large rotund frame wedged tightly between desk and office wall. The foxes he was referring to were my two rescued tame foxes Muffles and Velvet with himself being deputy head of Wirral Council's Parks and Open Spaces going by the name of Roger the Codger (*but not within earshot I hasten to add!*)

I was in his tiny, drab, nondescript office with its small vertical blind draped window overlooking the urban sprawl of Birkenhead in the middle of a third-floor corridor of Westminster House, the council's HQ. The reason for me being summoned to this rather cheerless environment was to discuss budgets, staffing and other matters relating to the general management of the Wirral Ranger Service in my capacity as Head Ranger.

Or at least that's what I thought!

A few months previous to this, his boss David Cooling, (*name slightly changed to protect the guilty and who also gets a mention in* From Badgers to Nighthawks*)* had now done a complete U-turn in his support of the Wirral Wildlife Rehabilitation Unit which my wife Ann and I had formed some years earlier.

Since it's early and somewhat accidental beginnings in 1984, the Unit had gained a fair amount of national and international interest due to its success in the care and rehabilitation of many species of wildlife from raptors, seabirds and numerous species of mammals, particularly badgers. One of the most publicised of these, both in the UK and abroad, was the rehabilitation of a member the nightjar family, a common nighthawk (*Chordeiles minor)* that was nursed back to health and released in Belize via the RAF and a VC10 aeroplane.

Due to the Unit's success in wildlife nursing and rehabilitation, I often found myself invited to present technical papers and lecture on the subject to various organisations including the Veterinary Nursing Association and vet students. Needless to say, Wirral Council deemed all this attention to be a great local authority public relations exercise and decided to give the Wildlife Rehabilitation Unit its official stamp of approval by adding Wildlife Officer to my job title. Not only did I have a new title bestowed upon me but more importantly the allocation of a small budget to allow me to procure the various necessary items such as medication and animal food etc. Before this I had to generate funds through talks and the kind generosity of the Wirral public often spurred on by the two local newspapers *The Wirral Globe* and *The Wirral News* who were always keen to run a story or two relating to some rescued creature or other.

The Unit also generated a fair amount of interest from television with me having been involved in the filming of programmes such as 'A Walk on the Wild Side' a thirty-minute documentary on the work of the Wildlife Rehabilitation Unit and 'The Animal Roadshow' presented by Desmond Morris which focused on my work with badgers plus 'Rolf's Amazing World of Animals' based around the hand rearing and rehabilitation of orphaned red squirrels.

I found the telly work interesting and quite surreal, but it could get a bit hectic at times with TV crews constantly filming something or other, plus the fact it was becoming the norm to have a well-known TV celebrity of the time around the place. Desmond Morris for instance spent time in the garden playing with a couple of boisterous badger cubs as did Simon King who spent an hour or two getting acquainted with Basil my tame boar badger. On another occasion Kim Wilde, daughter of the 1960's pop star Marty Wilde, who at the time was at the height of her own pop star career, sat drinking coffee in the living room whilst discussing the filming of another up and coming programme not related to music, but of her passion for wildlife with badgers being one of her favourites. Another figure to frequent the place was Mike McCartney (*Mike McGear*) of the chart-topping musical, comedy, and poetry trio The Scaffold. Mike not only became a great supporter of the Wildlife Rehab Unit but also a personal friend and he kindly wrote the foreword to my first book *From Badgers to Nighthawks*.

But the years were flowing by and despite the Unit still generating much publicity, the novelty of having a wildlife hospital-come-rehabilitation facility under the umbrella of the local authority was wearing a bit thin with one or two within the bubble of middle management who were now of the opinion that the council coffers could be better spent on something more productive. Unfortunately, the greatest negativity was coming from D. Cooling who, by this time, had by some miracle managed to claw himself up the greasy pole of promotion to reach the dizzy heights of Head of Parks and Open Spaces which included Cemeteries, Allotments, Parks & Gardens and unfortunately the Ranger Service!! And even more unfortunate was the fact that he was of the opinion that the Wildlife Rehabilitation Unit had been milked to its limit.

I couldn't help but contemplate that his lack of enthusiasm had arisen from one of the first tasks of his heady promotion when he summoned a meeting of various outdoor staff in the lecture theatre at Wirral Country Park Visitor Centre, Thurstaston, overlooking the Dee estuary and across to the hills of North Wales. Unfortunately, on the morning of the said meeting I received a frantic telephone call informing me that a male swan that I had rehabilitated some weeks previous had somehow got himself into a narrow steep sided channel and couldn't get out.

Obviously, my priority was to assist the swan rather than listen to the new Head of Parks and Open Spaces blathering on about how he was going to reorganise and streamline the department. As I was about to leave, the man himself came strolling down the long corridor of the visitor centre, dripping with self-importance, and enquired as to where I was going. He was rather taken aback at being informed that helping a swan took priority over listening to him prattling on and that I could attend one of his meetings anytime but would have only the one opportunity to assist the swan. Call me paranoid if you must but I couldn't help but come to the conclusion that his lack of enthusiasm for the Wildlife Rehab Unit just may have stemmed from this encounter and now he was wringing his hands in glee at the thought of payback!

But rumours were rife that budget cuts could be on the cards with the possibility of other ominously dark clouds drifting ever closer and he obviously saw this as the ideal opportunity to put an end to my wildlife escapades once and for all. As far as he was concerned my rescuing a swan or any other form of wildlife for that matter was over and done with and I was going back to wearing my Head Rangers hat albeit with more responsibility and a pay rise under the pretext of labelling it as promotion!

It was made quite clear that I would now be expected to concentrate all my efforts solely on managing the Ranger Service plus all the extra responsibilities that came with stepping onto the next rung of the pay scale. Now it was one thing to say that the Wildlife Rehab Unit no longer existed but quite another to put it into practise, particularly when members of the public still expected you to continue to care for sick and injured wildlife and the media still came knocking on the door.

The Unit's priority had always been successful rehabilitation often carried out over a period of many months as the kestrel, owl, badger, weasel, fox or whatever would begin a carefully controlled gradual soft release, but with the best will in the world it was inevitable that some animals would be beyond redemption, either through sickness, injury or humanisation. In these circumstances, for some at least, the kindest option was euthanasia but not all.

My foxes Muffles and Velvet were taken from the wild as tiny cubs, probably after their mother had been killed by fox hunters who knew of someone wanting a pet fox hence sparing them and as a consequence, they had been hand reared and were now far too humanised to even contemplate rehabilitation. They were two of the most adorable friendly animals you could ever wish to meet and were great ambassadors not only for their species, in having gone someway in dismissing some of the many misconceptions that abound about foxes, but also for the authority in having featured in many wildlife related TV programmes. Those of you who may have read *From Badgers to Nighthawks* will be familiar with the story of how Muffles and Velvet came to live out their lives at the Wildlife Rehab Unit and the joy they brought to all who met them, especially children.

Hence my being so stunned and totally gob-smacked at the question, "Malcolm! What are we going to do about these damn foxes?"

It took me a few seconds to get my head around what I considered to be a totally ludicrous question and responded with, "What do you mean what are we going to do with them?"

"Well, you are very busy managing the ranger service and we (*we being himself and D.C. his lord and master*) made it quite clear that after your promotion (*in inverted commas*) the Wildlife Rehabilitation Unit would cease to exist which obviously means no animals which of course includes your foxes."

I could feel the tension rising as I asked, "And what do you suggest I do with them?"

His reply knocked me for six as he quite seriously suggested that I should give them away followed by, "It doesn't really matter so long as they go."

I felt my blood pressure soar and my temper close to erupting at such a thoughtless and ridiculous comment as I angrily uttered the words, "Never in a million years!!" Followed by a few expletives that left him in no doubt as to what I thought of his suggestion.

He was clearly taken aback by my response as his large round face began to turn a rather alarming shade of scarlet and his grey walrus moustache and bushy eyebrows developed an uncontrollable twitch. His mouth opened in an attempt to speak but merely emitted some unintelligible sound, along with a fine spray of saliva to contaminate the confines of his tiny office as he attempted to put a little more space between us; but it was a futile attempt as his large frame was well and truly wedged betwixt desk and wall. I fired one more volley by telling him that if he seriously thought that I would even consider getting rid of my beloved foxes he could damn well think again! End of meeting!!!

Obviously with the plug having been pulled on the Unit's budget I was back to square one insofar as finances were concerned and it was inevitable that I had no choice but to wind things down tremendously not only from a financial point of view but also because my new responsibilities demanded a great deal more of my time and effort.

But thankfully the topic of getting rid of Muffles and Velvet was never mentioned again and they continued to live a contented life in their very large enclosure with its cosy wooden straw lined sleeping boxes and raised platforms where they could bask in the summer sun. They continued to enjoy their regular frolics around the adjacent, securely fenced wild paddock and as ever they were a joy to watch as they played catch me if you can as they vanished into the tall nettle beds to suddenly appear again to chase around over the rough grassland interspersed with thistles and vivid yellow buttercups and to prance upon the moss-covered logs. I say they, but in reality, Muffles was the one that tended to do the running. She was your typical picture postcard image of a fox with her rustic red coat and thick foxy brush whereas Velvet was much browner in colour and a little more rotund preferring to waddle rather than run!

Prior to coming to the Unit, she had been kept as a pet by a family in Liverpool living in a tiny shed with a small run attached in the back garden of a terraced house. Although much loved, she was fed on scraps and got very little exercise, hence being quite unfit and a little rotund. Despite improving her diet and carefully regulating her food intake, she remained on the plump side and much preferred to take life at a rather laid-back pace instead of charging around the place like a demented imp as the much sleeker and mischievous Muffles tended to do. Even though totally different in appearance, they shared the same gentle nature albeit with Muffles being the more outgoing of the two. They loved human company and liked nothing more than to have their tummies rubbed whilst their intelligent bright eyes stared warmly back at you and with mouth slightly open and tongue lolling to one side; they would give you their foxy grin of delight. Even though always gentle they were particularly so with children and gave many a child a foxy experience they would remember for the rest of their lives.

Mike McCartney introduced his own kids to them and even now after all these years they still have fond memories of meeting Muffles and Velvet as do many others. Some have since told me all these years later that the experience affected them greatly and that at the time they were going through a difficult period in their young lives. To this day they truly believe that Muffles and Velvet helped them tremendously in the healing process. I'm a great believer in the fact that animals, being so much more connected to the natural world, possess something magical that can help calm the damaged spirit of us mere mortals. Some of my most treasured memories are of the times I spent, particularly with Muffles, as I gently stroked her and she in turn would lick and gently nibble my arm whilst I gazed into those soft, intelligent, sparkling eyes to glimpse into her soul.

But, as with my own life, time was rolling on and Muffles and Velvet were getting on in years and beginning to show their age. Obviously, I knew they wouldn't live forever but tried not to dwell on such sad thoughts but on Saturday the 6th February 2010 the inevitable happened. It was a fine, clear, sunny morning, the daffodils were just coming into flower, and I had wandered down to their enclosure. Neither were to be seen and as I called them Muffles eventually made her way from the sleeping box to the pipe entrance. I was shocked at her appearance; it was though the years had suddenly caught her up overnight. I spoke quietly to her and as she slowly wandered over, I knew that her long life was coming to an end. An overwhelming feeling of sadness and loss came over me. She wasn't stumbling or falling over she just looked very old and tired. She followed me from the enclosure into the paddock where I placed a blanket on the grass for her to lie upon in the warmth of the winter sun and just sat with her. To have rushed her off to the vets would have been both pointless and cruel. She wasn't sick or injured, she was just very old and the last thing she needed was stress and as such I made the decision to let her pass away quietly and with dignity. She lay there throughout the day, she wasn't in pain or discomfort, she just wanted me to stay close to her. We spent our last few hours together before she finally closed her eyes for the last time. She was almost 15 years old, a grand old age for a fox!

Many years have passed since then and I still miss her. Some two months later Velvet also began to show signs of age catching up with her but unlike Muffles she was in discomfort, and I took her to the RSPCA's Stapely Grange Wildlife Hospital in Nantwich, Cheshire to be checked over by their vet. Unfortunately, the diagnosis wasn't good, her heart was giving up through old age and she recommended euthanasia. It was with a heavy heart that I drove her lifeless body home to be buried in the paddock next to Muffles.

Those two foxes had been a big part of my life for many years and had given so much joy to those fortunate enough to have met them. It was the end of an era, not just for the Wildlife Rehab Unit but for me also. Some may say, 'they were only foxes,' but to me they were far more than 'just foxes' they had character, they had spirit and they had souls and damn good ones at that!

My fascination with foxes along with badgers and otters goes back a long way, from reading about them as a kid in my well-thumbed copy of *The Observers Book of Wild Animals of the British Isles*. The memory of being totally spellbound by catching sight of my very first otter is as vivid now as way back then as is the time I caught a glimpse of a fox as it crept silently along the hedgerows during one of my many excursions into the nearby countryside from 21 Central Avenue, my mum and dad's three bedroomed semi-detached house situated on the Henthorn council estate on the outer fringes of Clitheroe.

I recall my feelings of sadness of seeing a young fox pacing up and down in its small grubby cage in the grounds of Clitheroe Castle for all and sundry to gaze at and torment along with a small aviary full of blue, yellow and green budgerigars twittering away as they fluttered from one white faeces covered perch to another whilst various breeds of rabbit miserably attempted to hop around in their tiny, stale, urine smelling hutches.

My next memorable fox encounter came many years later after we sold our little two up two down terraced house in Clitheroe to rent 1 Holme Head Cottage, Dunsop Bridge. The cottage was owned by the Duchy of Lancaster Estates and nestled deep in the valley of Whitendale within the Forest of Bowland, a designated Area of Outstanding Natural Beauty. I had just returned from enjoying a pint of ale and a game of dominoes whilst at the same time inhaling a mixture of sooty coal smoke wafting out of the open fire intermingled with the pungent aroma and pipe smoke of Jimmy Roscoe my doubles partner, his flat cap tilted at an angle and pipe clenched firmly between his teeth as he clutched his dominoes tightly to his chest.

All of these delights were only to be found on three nights a week in the salubrious confines of the tiny two up two down cottage that served as the Dunsop Bridge Working Men's Club. My final duty before retiring to my bed was to take Sally, our little rescued whippet down the track for her last constitutional. It was a very dark silent moonless night with a cold damp mist floating low over the land. Only the occasional *ke-wick, ke-wick* of a tawny owl calling to its mate through the darkness and the gentle gurgling of the river as it tumbled over rocks and boulders to join the River Hodder some half a mile or so downstream broke the silence. Now the river was subdued but during the heavy September rains or melting winter snow it quickly turned into a brown peat-stained torrent swelled by the deluge flowing from the hills to the Whitendale Valley far below.

As I made my way down the track Sally stayed close hesitant to stray too far in the blackness of the night and the beam of my torch struggling to penetrate the swirling mist drifting off the river. We hadn't gone far when through the mist I spotted what seemed to be two flickering eyes in the middle of the track slowly heading towards us. They were low to the ground and paused every now and again and seemed to move from left to right before moving on again. As they got closer, I stopped in the hope of catching whatever it was. For a few seconds, the beam of my torch penetrated the mist to reveal two shining red eyes which appeared to be totally devoid of any form and floating like some ghostly apparition over the track. Sally trembled with apprehension as she sniffed the night air for a scent and pricked her ears for a sound. As the thing got closer a shiver ran down my spine and the hairs at the back of my neck began to rise.

As it came closer it paused for a few seconds before heading off the track towards the river and the mist parted just enough to allow my beam to pick out the form of a very handsome dog fox in superb condition. He paused for a moment to glance towards the light before stealthily and silently vanishing into the misty darkness. Needless to say, I felt quite foolish in the fact that I hadn't instantly realised that the ghostly and seemingly bodiless apparition was nothing more than a fox on his nightly jaunts!

I wished him well and hoped he didn't fall prey to the beagle pack that hunted on foot along the steep heather slopes above.

On another occasion after once again returning quite late from enjoying a sooty pint in the DB Working Men's Club, I heard the distinctive whistle of the local gamekeeper calling his pheasants from the woods to their night roosting pen by the river. The only problem being that it was around midnight, and he had already done it! So, what or who was whistling?

Unlike my previous fox encounter, this time it was a clear bright moonlit night and as I made my way down the riverbank towards the sound and the pheasant pens, to my astonishment I clearly saw a fox sat outside the pen illuminated in the full moon. No one or anything else was to be seen. Had there been poachers around you wouldn't have seen the fox for dust. I watched for a minute or so. Eventually the fox stood up gave a stretch and a yawn and sauntered off. And the whistling stopped! *(Again, this is a tale I relate to in more detail in From Badgers to Nighthawks.)*

Was it the fox whistling? Well, communication plays a very important part of a fox's life with almost thirty groups of complex vocalisations having been documented but whistling isn't one of them! But there are many legends and folk tales out there relating to the foxes cunning and intelligence such as a fox collecting sheep's wool in his mouth and entering a stream, river, or pond. Once in the water he submerges with only his head above water whereupon all the fleas jump onto the wool to escape from drowning. He then releases the wool to float away along with the fleas! Or the story where he will sit nonchalantly and seemingly not at all interested in the rabbits that frolic around close by seemingly lulled into a sense of false security. But Reynard's cunning ploy works a treat as one ventures too close and then snap!! He's got his supper!

Foxes are opportunists and wired up to grab a meal whenever the opportunity arises, they have to be in order to survive and thankfully foxes are born survivors.

Muffles and Velvet were no different, despite being in captivity with good hearty meals always provided, the natural instinct was still there. For many years we kept free range chickens and when Muffles and Velvet were secured in their enclosure the chickens were allowed a free run of the fox paddock. It was quite a bizarre sight particularly on a warm summer's day to see half a dozen chickens sunning themselves next to two chilled out foxes separated only by half a centimetre of enclosure wire.

If I wished to let the foxes have the run of the paddock, I would first have to entice the chickens out with a bucket of grain and when the coast was clear, would close the paddock door and allow the foxes their freedom to chase and play. Unfortunately, on one occasion I had missed a chicken who had decided to ignore the rattling of my bucket and carry on scratching away hidden from view in the jungle of nettles. Muffles came charging out like a greyhound for her usual chase around the paddock and as she shot into the nettles I heard a loud shriek of panic from a chicken. Before I could dash to the rescue Muffles came racing out with the poor chicken firmly attached to her jaws!

I screamed at the top of my voice, "Muffles, put it down!" And to my astonishment she spit it out along with a few feathers and looked at me as if to say, "How did that get there?!!" Thankfully, the chicken was none the worse for the experience apart from the loss of a few tail feathers and a dent to its dignity.

Muffles and Velvet were not the only foxes around the place as every night we would put scraps of food out for a variety of wild creatures including hedgehogs and foxes with one very trusting little vixen standing out above the rest. When she first made an appearance is lost in the annals of time, but she would turn up every evening for her treats. Eventually she began to rest up during the day in a small copse of conifers by the house and Wildlife Rehab Unit. Over time she became so trusting that she would rest up on the edge of the trees in full view. I would go about my business coming and going from the house to the Unit often passing but a few metres from her and she would just lie there totally relaxed quietly watching me. One year in early March we didn't see her for some time and were worried that something untoward may have happened but to our relief she turned up one day in the middle of April with her teats swollen and full of milk. We now of course realised the reason for her absence, she had given birth and was suckling tiny chocolate brown cubs. But the biggest thrill and proof of complete and utter trust was one evening some weeks later when she brought them along for us to see.

Another year as I was about to go into a shed that at the time served as the Wildlife Rehabs hospital unit, I heard the unmistakable barking of tiny fox cubs and as I shone a torch under the raised floor three pairs of eyes stared back at me. She had moved her cubs from the natal den to under the raised floor of the shed. One of my favourite photos is one I took of her on a sunny early April day as she stood amongst the daffodils on the edge of the little conifer copse. She was once again heavy with milk, and I remember thinking that she looked a little thin and tired. Sadly, that was the last time we ever saw her. We could only speculate as to why we never saw her again, but she was getting on in years and perhaps the burden of raising a family at her age proved too much. Unfortunately, her death would have put a great burden on her mate the dog fox as he attempted to provide for himself and the cubs. I hope he succeeded!

It's an amazing privilege to gain the total trust of a truly wild creature and for them to regard you as part and parcel of their environment. Over the years we hand reared numerous orphaned wild creatures and nursed back to health many sick or injured adult ones. The hand rearing and nursing, despite the 24/7 hours, was the easy bit, successful rehabilitation was the difficult part, get it wrong and all your hard work was for nothing and could easily result in the slow death of the creature you were trying to help either through starvation, predation, or injury. With some creatures it could involve weeks of pre-release preparation followed by many more weeks or even months of after release care including supplementary feeding and monitoring to ensure that the animal was coping well and integrating back into the society of its species. I could write endless chapters on the ins and outs of successful rehabilitation from badgers to peregrine falcons. Sometimes it can be fairly straightforward with others being much more difficult depending on the species and the reason for them finding themselves in captivity in the first place. There is so much to take into consideration such as correctly assessing the animal's suitability for successful rehabilitation followed by surveying the habitat of a proposed release site for food availability plus any potential risk of inter species territorial disputes or human conflict etc.

But this isn't a book about the ins and outs of wildlife rehabilitation but a story of my experiences of working with and around wildlife and as Mr D. Cooling and Roger the Codger insisted on drilling into me the Wirral Wildlife Rehabilitation Unit was drawing to a close with (*officially at least*) never another creature to pass through its door. It was the end of an era, the end of something that had taken over not just my life but also that of my wife Ann's. She was still working as a vet nurse and I, in inverted commas, had been promoted!

I must confess that for a while at least I actually enjoyed the extra responsibility and put my heart and soul into it and took great satisfaction in the fact that Wirral's country parks began to gain the prestigious Green Flag awards under my watch. The first being Wirral Country Park at Thurstaston with Mike McCartney kindly accepting the invitation to be guest of honour at the award ceremony.

Despite the Wildlife Rehab Unit no longer being part of the council and attached to my official duties, the odd creature or two did manage to sneak past the noses of D. C. and R.C. and of course the many memories could never be taken away particularly with regards to some of the more amusing incidents and animal characters to be told in the next chapter.

2

Fred Retains His Crown Jewels, A Seal In Custody & An Eagle Owl In A Bag.

In *From Badgers to Nighthawks* I told the tale of myself, the RSPCA and a vet attempting to catch a muntjac deer in the middle of Birkenhead, and the merry dance it led us as it bounded from garden to garden and of it shredding RSPCA Inspector Fred Armstrong's brand new catching net as he attempted to swoop it up as it shot past him like an Exocet missile on legs. But with so many stories it's impossible to tell them all at one sitting with many having to be stored away for another day. One such story once again involved RSPCA Inspector Fred Armstrong, not with a deer this time but a very large bull Atlantic grey seal!

Off the coast of West Kirby on the Wirral Peninsula and at the mouth of the Dee Estuary bordering England and North Wales lies an archipelago of three small islands, Little Eye, Middle Eye and the largest, Hilbre Island, all falling under my brief as Wirral Council's Head Ranger and Wildlife Officer.

The islands are designated a Local Nature Reserve, a Site of Special Scientific Interest, a Special Area of Conservation, and a Ramsar Site under the Ramsar Convention of Wetlands of International Importance. Needless to say, with such an impressive array of designations it goes without saying that the place abounds with wildlife with everything from thousands of wintering waders, spring and summer migrants to raptors and mammals with everything from wood mouse to otter having been recorded.

Over the years an impressive array of marine mammals has also been recorded with Atlantic grey seals, harbour and common porpoise, bottlenose dolphin and even the occasional whale! *(I was once alerted to a beached bottlenose whale on the beach at Thurstaston which sadly died due to severe injuries suspected to have been caused by having been tangled in commercial fishing nets.)* The islands only buildings are situated on the main island and consist of the remains of the old lifeboat station and slipway, the old Buoy Masters house, store and workshop, a wooden building used by the Mersey Canoe Club, another by Hilbre Bird Observatory, two privately owned cottages, the Telegraph Station and finally the old Telegraph House occupied at the time by the islands only permanent resident, the Hilbre Ranger.

The post became non-residential in 2011 due to a combination of factors but primarily as a council cost cutting exercise coupled with the logistics of having a ranger living permanently on the island with a life dominated by the tides and last but not least the isolation eventually sent most of them a little loopy with an overwhelming tendency to do some very strange things.

It was rumoured that one individual on a full moon or winter solstice would dance around the island stark naked whilst swinging a storm lamp and singing, 'The Light is Returning' at the top of their voice. It was also said that on a still clear night the flickering of the lamp could be seen across the sands in West Kirby whilst the haunting dulcet tones drifted eerily through the night air. Just how true the story is I cannot say or if it was indeed the ranger and not some mystical lost soul rejoicing in the joys and mysteries of nature and the heavens. Anyway, enough of that, back to the story in hand.

With such a vast diversity of wildlife it was inevitable that occasionally either the ranger *(when not skipping around naked!)* or a member of the public would come across some creature or other in need of help. Usually, it would be a wader or a seagull but occasionally it would be an Atlantic grey seal from the colony of around five hundred or more that frequent the waters around the islands who at low tide, would haul out onto a sand bank known as the West Hoyle Bank.

On this occasion it was a very large bull seal that Fred and I were planning to release by the old lifeboat slipway on the far side of Hilbre. I had released quite a few seals there before as it was an ideal location in that they could waddle down the slipway into the sea observed by more of their kind as their large roman nosed heads bobbed out of the water curious as to what was going on. Normally it was a straightforward operation with the seal firmly encased in a specially designed stretcher to restrict its movements during transit. But this was a very large seal and the journey from West Kirby across to the islands can be very bumpy, particularly when you leave the sand behind which in itself can be rather like driving over corrugated sheeting to eventually drive over the seaweed encrusted rocks.

With all hands to the task, we eventually lifted the great bulk of the seal into the back of the Hilbre ranger's Land Rover and with Fred and I squeezed either side of it and with our bottoms perched precariously on the long narrow green seats, off we went. At first everything was fine as we sped along, the sand still wet with the receding tide, the salty spray, and the smell of the sea wafting in from the open canvas back. We were about halfway across when the great grey bulk became a little restless and decided to attempt to wriggle its way out of the stretcher. Now there was very little room in the back of the vehicle and as the seal became more and more active, Fred and I had to shuffle our legs up and down and from left to right to avoid them being crushed by the great hulk of a beast. We had just left the relative smoothness of the sand and paused momentarily to engage four-wheel drive to carefully manoeuvre us over and around the slippery seaweed strewn rocks. The Land Rover pitched from side to side as it crawled along at a snail's pace with Fred and I hanging on to whatever we could to stop ourselves from either being tipped out of the back into a salty rock pool or worse still, falling on top of the now very restless monster. And then it happened!

Suddenly we lurched violently to the left and as we did so the seal having gained a little more thrust managed to wriggle and squirm just enough to get its head and shoulders almost out of the stretcher. Unfortunately, Fred also gained a little more forward thrust and began to slide off his seat with legs and feet frantically thrashing wildly in search of a foothold in order to stop himself being propelled onto the back of what was by now one not very amused very large lump of writhing blubber!

As poor Fred slid ever more forward and with legs wide apart the seal, not wishing to miss such an opportunity and with mouth agape, made a lunge for his manhood!! Poor Fred let out a shrill scream of terror whilst at the same time finally finding the reverse thrust to propel him backwards as far as the lack of space would allow as the seal's jaws snapped shut with a sickening crunch. Mercifully due to another lurch to the left the seal didn't quite reach its target and Fred narrowly avoided his voice gaining quite a few octaves by the skin of his teeth! Needless to say, we decided to abandon ship (*Land Rover*) and follow on behind on foot, not only for our safety but also because poor Fred was in dire need of the sea air to cool his perspiration and bring the colour back to his cheeks. Eventually we arrived on the island without further mishap and albeit with a bit of a tussle we eventually managed to return the writhing monster back to the deep!

Whilst on the subject of seals, I got a telephone call one day from Wallasey police station where a rather flustered desk sergeant informed me that they had a young seal in one of their cells and could I go and collect it? Apparently, a guy walking his dog on the beach at New Brighton came across a seal pup and, in his wisdom, decided it was in dire need of rescue whereupon he wrapped it in his jacket, put it into the boot of his car and trundled it off to Wallasey nick. Unfortunately, rescue was the last thing it needed or wanted! Grey seals haul themselves ashore to give birth to a single pup covered in fluffy white fur during autumn and winter. The female suckles the pup with her rich high fat content milk every 5 or 6 hours for around three weeks after which, the pup has trebled in weight, is fully weaned, and moulted out of its white baby coat. From now it has to live off its fat reserves until adept at catching fish and will often lie up alone on a beach or rocks. But as with fledgling birds, leverets, fox cubs and many other young animals, some well- meaning human stumbles across them and carries them off under the assumption that they have been abandoned. Every year animal rescue centres are inundated with such creatures but to be carted off in the boot of a car and incarcerated in a police cell is something else!

Anyway, off I went to collect the pup and on arrival at the station I was taken down a long, narrow corridor, its drab grey painted walls now flaking and stained. On we went past equally gloomy grey steel doors until finally the sergeant said, 'It's in here.'

The door creaked open to reveal a small windowless cell. To the left was a bed, its mattress encased in a dark blue plastic cover, on the opposite side a white plastic chair, a tiny sink with a constantly dripping tap and a stainless-steel loo minus seat. Posters adorned the cold white tiled walls informing the occupants of their legal rights and the danger of drugs etc., and there on the dark red painted concrete floor was the seal pup, its white fur now a silvery grey. Its enormous black eyes stared up at me as it waddled towards me bleating sorrowfully. It was obviously not long weaned and confused as to why its mother who had been so caring and attentive had now suddenly abandoned it.

I quickly wrapped it in a blanket and placed in the back of my Land Rover for the twenty-minute drive to the Unit to be weighed and examined. It was uninjured but a little underweight for a pup of its age and obviously hungry as it didn't hesitate in the slightest when given the chance to gulp down a few herrings. Luckily, we had a very large aviary equipped with a good-sized pool that could accommodate it until it had gained sufficient weight to be released. I would go in two or three times a day armed with a bucket of fresh fish from Birkenhead market whereupon it would immediately give out its pathetic bleating call and come waddling over, its big round eyes glistening like two shiny black marbles.

Thankfully, it gained weight quickly with enough fat reserves to think about release and within a few short weeks, like the big bull seal, was soon in the back of a Land Rover heading out to Hilbre Island, not sheathed in a stretcher like the bull seal but in a fiberglass animal carrier. Once reaching the island we carried the carrier over the uneven red sandstone rocks and crevices to the old lifeboat slipway. The sea was calm and gently lapping over the old slipway. Dark green tentacles of seaweed lazily rising and falling caressing the old stone as they slipped back into the sea. Once again, the large roman nosed heads of Atlantic grey seals began bobbing out of the water curious as to what we were doing, there one minute and gone the next only to pop up again somewhere else. I slid open the carrier door and tentatively the pup emerged. It looked around for a few moments and with nostrils and whiskers twitching took in the salty air.

After what seemed an age, it eventually waddled its way towards the water's edge and satisfied that all was going well I picked up the now empty carrier and began to make my way back up the slipway confident that when I turned around the pup would have joined the throng of bobbing seal heads. But I hadn't gone far when I heard the slap, slap of flippers on concrete followed by the now familiar sorrowful cries of the pup and as I turned to look back, he was waddling back up the slipway behind me. All I could do was to perch my bum on the carrier in the hope that eventually the smell of the sea and the presence of his own kind would lure him away. Finally, as he cast a last gaze towards me with those big dark eyes, he waddled down the slipway, slipped into the sea and was gone.

On another occasion I got a call from Birkenhead police station explaining that whilst patrolling Birkenhead Park officers had spotted a couple of youths by the Lilly Lobe Bridge spanning the Lower Lake who appeared to be struggling to carry a very large black holdall that every now and then appeared to wriggle and squirm as if alive.

As the officers approached to investigate the youths apparently exclaimed in a guttural North End of Birkenhead accent, 'It's the coppers!'

Whereupon they immediately abandoned the holdall to make off hotly pursued by the officers only to vanish through the Grand Entrance archway and off down Park Road East never to be seen again. Eventually after a futile chase the breathless and perspiration browed officers returned to retrieve the holdall that by now was in the process of wriggling its way down a footpath like a giant black slug! Backup was duly summoned in the form of a police vehicle to transport the 'thing' to Birkenhead nick.

Apparently, the short drive to the station wasn't without its moments as the bumping, scraping and scratching sounds coming from the boot caused the driver to worry that whatever was in there would at any moment claw its way out of the bag and through the upholstery of the rear seats to join him. But thankfully the holdall stood up to the onslaught and was duly secured in a storeroom.

Then I got the call! 'Malcolm, Birkenhead nick here, any chance you can get over ASAP? We've got a damn big black holdall bouncing all over a storeroom floor, God knows what's inside, but it's not amused!'

'OK,' I replied, 'I'll be there in half an hour.'

As I entered the station the desk sergeant quickly ushered me through a door and down a passageway into a windowless storeroom. As we entered, he flicked a switch to illuminate a single cobwebbed adorned lightbulb to cast its dim glow around the room. It was crammed full of old filing cabinets and desks, one of which was being used to prop up some coppers transport in the form of a bicycle with a pair of cycle clips adorning the handlebars. A mountain of faded brown cardboard storage boxes some bursting at the seams with files and papers were stacked in a corner from floor to ceiling.

As my brain attempted to take in the disarray, the sergeant, pointing towards an old metal dark green filing cabinet exclaimed, 'It's over there.'

As I followed the line of his trembling finger, I spotted a large black holdall rocking slowly from side to side.

'Have you looked inside?' I enquired.

'Not on your nelly, that's your job,' he retorted, obviously attempting to regain at least some form of authority.

At this point I asked him to close the door as I pulled on my thick animal handling gloves. In reality they were in fact barbecue gloves to protect one from hot coals, but they served the purpose and afforded some protection at least from sharp teeth and slashing claws, albeit more psychological than in practise. Anyway, with gloves adorned I proceeded to fumble with the holdalls large brass zip and very slowly began to draw it back a little to take a peek inside as the sergeant prepared himself for a hasty retreat by the door. The holdall bounced and jumped as whatever was inside primed itself for freedom. Slowly I pulled back the zip. It was awkward and stiff not helped by the inflexibility of my gloves but slowly and surely the holdall began to open and as it did so a large tawny brown head with two erect ear-tufts popped out as if out of a Jack-In-The-Box with two enormous orange fiery eyes staring back at me.

It was a very large female European Eagle Owl (*Bubo bubo*), and she wasn't amused!! Much to the relief of the sergeant I rapidly but gently pushed the horned head back from whence it came and zipped her up again deciding to check her out properly once back at the Wildlife Rehab Unit. Some thirty minutes later the holdall was sat or to be more precise bouncing around the floor of the Units new fully equipped log cabin that now served as a hospital and recuperation facility. *(A replacement for the old shed that the fox cubs were under.)* With windows and door tightly shut I once more donned my gloves and proceeded to unzip the holdall but at least this time I knew what was inside!

Slowly but surely the zip slid back until once again the tawny brown tufted eared and orange eyed head popped out followed by its broad shoulders. Its big powerful black curved beak loudly clicked away in a mixture of fear and anger as it glowered at me. Somehow, I needed to restrain it before it had the chance to completely wriggle out and crash around the place in a blind panic. Luckily, I was able to open the holdall up just enough in order for me to restrain its wings and slowly wriggle it free of the holdall. Once fully out I could see that it was wearing leather anklets with leather straps threaded through brass eyelets. These are known as jesses in the falconry world and used by falconers to grip or thread a swivel through cut out slits in order to attach a leash whilst the bird is sat on the falconer's arm. This made life much easier and in one quick movement I grabbed the jesses with my gloved left hand whilst lifting the owl onto my arm with my right.

Thankfully, the gloves extended quite a way up the forearm affording me some protection from those enormous feet armed with equally enormous, long black powerful talons. Of course she didn't just sit there contentedly admiring her new surroundings! Just the opposite in fact as she constantly attempted to fly off (*known as baiting*) with the draught off her six-foot wingspan causing mayhem not to mention battering my head. With my left hand gripping her jesses as tightly as my thick clumsy gloves would allow, I placed my right hand on her chest to gently lift her back onto my arm where once again I would feel the vice like grip of her enormous feet and her long black talons penetrating the leather.

Finally, after some thirty minutes or so of gentleness and soothing words she slowly ceased her panting, and her expression of fear and anger began to diminish until eventually with my arm sagging under her enormous weight, she allowed me to gently stroke her breast. A female European Eagle Owl can stand 75 cm (*around 29 inches*) tall and weigh in at around 4 kilos (*8 lbs*) with a wingspan of 188 cm (*6 feet*) and this owl stretched all of those statistics to their limit!! By now I was satisfied that thankfully she wasn't injured and appeared to be in good physical condition and with a leash securely attached to her jesses I carried her outside and popped her into a large aviary to recover from her ordeal.

She settled in well and was soon tucking into a meal and exploring her new surroundings, and that evening we could hear her distinctive deep call of *oohu-oohu-oohu* as she perched to gaze out beyond the confines of the aviary. A local newspaper did a story on her ordeal resulting in her owner contacting the police who in turn informed me that she would be going home. Apparently, she lived in an aviary in his back garden deep in the urbanised jungle of Birkenhead until one night someone broke in and stole her. Being mainly nocturnal she would of course have been quite alert and active and how they managed to restrain her to unceremoniously stuff her into the holdall beggar's belief.

The following morning one very relieved owner called round to collect her and take her home. Despite her intimidating size she was quite a pleasant bird and obviously accustomed to being handled. Presumably, the youths in Birkenhead Park were the culprits but what on earth they planned to do with her was anybody's guess?

Even more bizarre was the fact that our paths would cross again in the not-too-distant future as she was abducted on at least two more occasions each time finding her way back to me only to be collected again to be not so safely secured in her burglar friendly aviary.

The original abductors were never found and escaped the wrath of the law but it's somewhat consoling to fantasise that one night they broke into an enclosure that housed not a bird but a very large and not so friendly very hungry grizzly bear. If only!!

Before we leave the subject of eagle owls there is one last tale I must tell!

It was around 10 am and I was in the process of cleaning out the hospital pen of a hedgehog, not one of my favourite occupations for as cute as they are, they are also award-winning pooing machines! They seem to take great delight in pooing and then pooing even more with the final indignation for the carer being that they now walk through it and smear it everywhere! Mucky little devils!!

Anyway, I was just peeling off my bright yellow marigolds now streaked with brown hedgehog poo when the telephone rang. I picked up the receiver to be informed by the receptionist at the Wirral Country Park Visitor Centre that a gentleman had rung to say that a very large owl had been sat at the top of a telegraph pole for a week and could I give him a ring. So, without further ado, I dialled the number and almost immediately a gentleman answered. I explained who I was and enquired as to how I could be of help, he sounded quite agitated as he went to great lengths to explain that this big owl had been perched at the top of this telegraph pole for over a week and hadn't moved a muscle.

I asked a few questions in an effort to determine the situation, but his impatience became quite acute as he retorted, 'Will you listen, it's there now, I can see it from my living room window, will you come and rescue it?'

By this time, I had gleaned enough information from him to be pretty well convinced that his owl was in fact a large plastic decoy put there by whoever for whatever purpose. You should have heard the expletives when I endeavoured to explain this to him!! He was not amused and very indignant at my assumption that he could possibly mistake a big grey plastic owl for the real thing. Anyway, to cut a long story short, I finally agreed to go along if only to humour him and off I went. As I arrived, he was standing by the garden gate, and it was pretty obvious by his demeanour that I was not flavour of the month.

As I got out of the Land Rover my feet had hardly touched the tarmac before he was upon me and with one hand on my shoulder, he pointed with the other to the telegraph pole across the road exclaiming, "There it is, now do you damn well believe me? The poor bugger must be starving, it hasn't moved for over a week."

As soon as I gazed at the creature through my binoculars it was obvious that my original assumption was correct which of course put me in a bit of a quandary as to how I was going to convince him that it was indeed a big lump of plastic in the form of a large owl and not, as he believed, a living, breathing creature in dire need of rescue! Finally, I handed him my binoculars and invited him to take a look for himself. He raised the glasses to his eyes then lowered them again before raising them one more time to take a second and longer look. He uttered not a sound, but his body language spoke volumes. At last, the silence was broken as he thrust the binoculars into my chest whilst muttering a few incomprehensible expletives and turned tail to trot off back down the garden path to vanish into the house giving the door an almighty slam behind him. With a last look at the big lump of grey plastic and an unbelieving shake of my head I headed for home. I like to think that his rudeness was simply his way of hiding his embarrassment at being so easily taken in but in reality, I tend to think that he was just plain arrogant and didn't have the bottle to admit his mistake or appreciate the humour of it all. But in his defence, he was genuinely concerned for what he believed to be a creature in need.

3

A Swan with Attitude, A Talking Raven & Bert the Buzzard

In Chapter One, I related the tale of my ruffling the feathers of the newly promoted Mr D. Cooling when I regarded going to the aid of a swan more important than listening to him prattling on about how he was going to rejuvenate and streamline the ranger service in his capacity as the newly appointed Head of Parks and Open Spaces. The swan in question was a rather large, very handsome and more often than not, very stroppy cob (*male*) mute swan who found his way into the Unit via the RSPCA. I forget the exact circumstances of his rescue, but I do remember him still being a juvenile with brown feathers intermingled with white. He wasn't sick or injured but he was on the skinny side and in need of a bit of care and attention. He was quite friendly and eagerly accepted any offerings of food and as such we immediately housed him in the large seabird aviary with its fairly large deep pool. (*The same one that the seal pup had previously occupied.*) A couple of weeks went by in which time he had settled in well and gained weight when another call came from the RSPCA asking if we could take a second swan, this time a pen (*female*) of around the same age that was apparently found dodging traffic on the central reservation of the M53 motorway!

She was in a much poorer state than the cob and as such needed more care and it was pretty obvious that it was going to take quite some time to get her fit again meaning that any thought of release would in all probability be quite some time off. She wasn't as sociable as the cob and to help her settle we decided that she should share the seabird aviary with him, it was love at first sight! It was quite emotional to watch as they waddled over to each other giving off plaintive little squeaks followed by mutual preening and entwining of necks. The cob quickly began to regain his strength but as we expected she was taking much longer and as time went on, they were obviously getting bigger and as such I took the decision to allow them to have the freedom to wander around the place and only be secured in the aviary during the night.

This worked a treat as it allowed them much more space to exercise their wings and graze the grass of Muffles and Velvets paddock (*of course not whilst Muffles and Velvet were chasing around it like a couple of demented imps!*) It was a comical sight to see two large swans sharing a paddock with chickens and goats, yes goats! We not only kept free range chickens, but we also had four goats Polly, Jasmine, Candy, and Winkle. The goats would be grazing or messing about playfully head butting each other or just generally lazing about the place chewing their cud, the chickens scratched around doing the comical things that chickens do whilst the swans busied themselves preening their long feathers or with a loud whooshing of wind enthusiastically flapping their enormous wings all to be watched over by two chilled out foxes lazily lounging around on the raised platforms within their enclosure. Allowing the swans to have a free run of the place was great but it did have its drawbacks, particularly as far as the cob was concerned. He was maturing into a fine specimen, now almost pure white and with his grey bill turning an orangey pink and he was big! Not just big, but big with attitude!

Many was the time I would be walking down the long, wide grassy strip of land with various aviaries and enclosures on either side when I would hear the unmistakable whoosh, whoosh, whoosh of wings rapidly descending down upon me from behind and as I turned to face my attacker the great white beast would be coming at me like a steam train whereupon at the last minute he would slam on the brakes to come to a skidding halt a mere six inches from me. If that wasn't intimidating enough, he would then virtually stand on tiptoe and stretch up his long neck in order to make himself as tall and as threatening as he possibly could.

Now I'm not very tall (*some would even have the audacity to say vertically challenged!*) so as you can imagine it didn't take an awful lot of stretching for him to be peering down upon me! If that wasn't enough, he would then puff out his chest and issue a few menacing hisses whilst at the same time spreading out his massive powerful wings in preparation to give me an almighty whack on the thigh. Obviously, it stung a bit and as I was walking up and down all the time I was constantly on my guard in anticipation of the next assault. Eventually I came to the conclusion that there was only one thing for it, I had to stand up to him and let him know in no uncertain terms that I was the boss. After all he was only a swan, albeit a damn big one, but in the past I had been bitten and peed on by a fox, lunged at and had my wellies shredded, not to mention my thumb merrily chewed by a badger and on occasions had the need to wrench some bird of prey's talons from beneath my skin, so a swan shouldn't pause too much of a problem. And so it was that the next time I walked down the long wide grassy stretch to hear the sound of rapidly beating wings descending down upon me I once again turned to face my attacker.

Closer and closer he came, wings whoosh, whoosh, whooshing for all their worth. I stood my ground; he slammed on the brakes to come skidding towards me almost beak to nose and then I pounced! Before he knew what was happening and with the speed and dexterity of a Ninja warrior, I was behind him and with arms outstretched I gripped his wings to quickly fold them firmly but gently back to his side whereupon I picked him up and tucked his great white bulk under my arm. The transformation was magical!! If he could have cried, he would have done, but instead he let out the most pathetic high-pitched squeaks of 'put me down.' You really wouldn't have believed that such a feeble sound could have come from such big powerful bird. Rather than let him go there and then I walked around with him tucked under my arm with both hands and arms restraining his wings until eventually I let him go. To say he sulked would be an understatement as he dejectedly shuffled off with his back arched, his head hanging low and his wing tips almost dragging on the floor. Elated at my victory I thought 'Well that taught him a lesson he won't forget in a hurry, and he'll think twice before trying that again!' But as I was to quickly discover, he suffered from short term memory loss!!

Only a few short days later whilst wandering down to check on Hamish, my Scottish Wildcat, I once again heard the menacing whoosh, whoosh, whooshing of mighty wing beats as he came charging down on me. I turned, he braked with his great black webbed feet skidding to a halt only a few inches from me and wings poised ready to give me an almighty whack. Once again, I brought my martial art skills into play and much to his disgust proceeded to overpower him, tuck him under my arm and carried him around for ten minutes or so whilst he once again emitted his pathetic little squeaks. As time went on, we developed an almost mutual respect, but he never quite got over the irresistible urge to try it on. She on the other hand, the love of his life, was just the opposite and always as gentle as a lamb.

Now it was one thing for him to have a go at me, after all we were now on reasonably good terms and even beginning to consider our occasional skirmishes as nothing more than a bit of a game between friends. But to someone who didn't know him and totally unaccustomed to being eyeballed by a giant swan his antics could be pretty alarming. To make matters worse he also had a warped sense of humour in that if I was showing someone around the place he would be doubly intimidating, but not to me! He would focus all his finely honed skills of terrorisation on the stranger and I, rather guiltily must confess to finding his antics rather amusing.

On one occasion I was showing a television producer around the place in preparation for the filming of a documentary and we were standing by the Scottish wildcat enclosure, home to Hamish my pure-bred male and awe inspiring wildcat discussing the possibility of filming him, when once again I heard the now very familiar whoosh, whoosh, whoosh of beating wings.

The producer turned towards the sound to see a great white swan coming towards him like a steam train, the colour drained from his face as he stuttered 'What the!!!' and as he turned to make his escape towards Muffles and Velvets paddock, I grabbed his arm and assured him that all would be well.

'Just stand your ground,' I advised 'He's fine, you will be ok.'

As the cob got within a couple of feet away, he applied the brakes to come skidding to a halt to show off his full and by now finally tuned skills of intimidation. Not at me this time but to the poor producer who, with ashen face and stuttered words, attempted to continue with our discussion whilst being eyeballed by one very large swan with wings outstretched and poised to deliver an almighty blow. But the blow wasn't forthcoming, not for now at least! He was milking the occasion for all it was worth and appeared to be truly relishing in his prolonged act of terrorisation. Every now and again I would put myself between him and his quarry but to no avail as he merely side stepped around me to continue his game.

By this time, the poor bloke was beginning to perspire with beads of sweat forming droplets on his clammy forehead. Hamish who by now was calmly sitting on his platform watching all of this with what I can only conclude to be the feline equivalent of a bemused expression.

Once again, I attempted to offer some form of reassurance to calm his nerves as I said, 'Look don't worry, he's only checking you out he does this with everybody.' At last, the poor guy appeared to relax a little and even apologised saying that he just wasn't accustomed to being given the once over by a swan.

'Just ignore him and let's get on with planning the filming,' I advised.

To give credit where credit's due, he tried his best but as we gazed through the green diamond mesh of Hamish's enclosure the cob played his trump card and with an almighty whack of a wing landed a stinging blow onto the producer's thigh! Ouch!!! All I could do was apologise and unceremoniously return the victor to the confines of his aviary, at least until the producer had finished his reconnoitre of the place and concluded his plans for the forthcoming filming.

With all done and a promise that the cob would be confined to barracks during filming he limped back to his car and bid farewell. I suppose in hindsight I should have had him safely confined in the first place but as I said before, I couldn't help but find his antics amusing and he did enjoy his little games! Time rolled on and the swans were by now well and truly ready for rehabilitation, but the problem was where to release them? Swans, cobs in particular, can be very territorial and fiercely battle with intruders to drive them away or even kill them meaning that we had to choose a release site extremely carefully. It was crucial that we would be able to monitor them for at least a few weeks after release whereupon if a problem arose, we would be on hand to help.

Eventually we were offered a fantastic release site by a converted old watermill with a large private lake fed by a meandering stream and no other swans to worry about. Once we were happy that the site was indeed just what we were looking for we made plans for their release and two weeks later with the pair of them sat comfortably in the back of my van wrapped in their swan bags, (*Special bags designed to restrain swans for carrying and transporting*) off we went.

The journey took about an hour and was thankfully totally uneventful with the swans seemingly calm and happy. On arrival at the lake, we carried them encased in their bright red bags to the water's edge and slowly unpeeled the Velcro straps to allow them their freedom.

The cob was the first to step out, he looked around for a minute or two before shaking his enormous bulk to straighten out his ruffled feathers and then the moment we had been waiting for as he waddled over to the water's edge, took a long drink and waded in. He was in seventh heaven and even more so when within a few minutes the pen joined him. They were a joy to watch as they splashed around, their great white wings sending sprays of water to drop around them like clear transparent jewels forming ever increasing circles of ripples to spread out around them. Eventually they began to explore their new surroundings but never wandering too far. They were so graceful as they sedately drifted from one spot to the next leaving a wake on the surface to gently spread out behind them. Slowly but surely their explorations brought them back to the lake side to sail beneath the shadow of a weeping willow tree, its branches like long slender green tentacles caressing the surface. Here they paused to completely submerge their long slender necks to sift through the weed and gravel below.

It was difficult to believe that these were our swans, particularly the cob who had now morphed from being a large intimidating beast of a thing with thrashing wings into a creature of graceful beauty. We stayed to watch them for ages before saying our goodbyes, but not final goodbyes as we would be back the following day and for many more days and weeks to come. As time passed, they became ever more adventurous until eventually they were familiar with every inch of the lake and its little inlets and grassy verges.

But one day the cob became just a little too adventurous! He decided to inspect the green moss and fern encrusted old oak sluice gate that in times past would have been raised to allow a torrent of water to flow under the mill to drive the machinery to grind the corn. But that was many years ago, and now the mill had been converted into a home with the gate no longer opened. However, due to the lake being fed by a stream, water still flowed over it to tumble into a narrow canal running under the old mill to remerge on the far side where it continued for some way before its vertical grey stone and moss encrusted sides merged into a gently sloping grassy bank where it continued as a meandering little stream. We aren't quite sure how, but somehow, he managed to tumble over the sluice gate with his only way of escape being to paddle his way through the dark wet tunnel under the mill to finally return to daylight only to find himself stuck in the narrow canal, so narrow in fact that he couldn't even stretch out his wings.

He was of course totally disorientated with no idea as how to return to the lake or even escape from the tall, sided canal. Thankfully, the residents of the mill had witnessed his predicament and immediately got on the telephone to the Country Park Visitor Centre at Thurstaston to inform me of the dilemma and could I rescue him?!

Now this is where the tale takes us right back to the beginning whereupon I ruffle the feathers of the newly appointed Head of Parks and Open Spaces, Mr D. Cooling (*once again the name changed ever so slightly to protect the guilty!*) as I duly informed him that rescuing a swan took priority over listening to him prattling on about his bizarre ideas for streamlining the ranger service. As I left a rather flustered and crimson faced D. Cooling standing dejected in the corridor to cool off (*No pun intended!*) I shot off to the rescue.

When I finally arrived, the cob was paddling up and down not knowing what to do. The narrowness and steep sides of the canal left him with no alternative but to walk his way out until he came to the grassy bank, but he was obviously reluctant to do this. His only thought was to get back to the lake and his mate and as far as he was concerned the only way to do that was to go back under the mill and somehow attempt to get back over the sluice gate. But of course, that was impossible, the gate was too high and there was certainly no room for him to flap his great wings in an attempt to fly up and over. Quickly I weighed up the situation and came to the conclusion that I had no alternative but to get in there with him and either guide him or carry him out.

The easiest way for me to join him was to walk through a field directly behind the mill until I came to the grassy bank at the end of the canal whereupon I could enter the water and make my way towards him. Thankfully, it was only ankle deep with the high stone sides green and slimy with mosses clinging to the damp brickwork, whilst ferns sprouted from cracks and crevices. I had to wade quite a way before I got close to him as he hadn't wandered far from where he first came out from under the mill. He made a woeful sight as he unhappily paddled up and down obviously stressed and confused by his ordeal. As I got closer, he spotted me and instantly appeared to recognise me as he came paddling towards me, his bulk of a frame ungainly rocking from side to side as his great black webbed feet splashed away in the shallow water.

Once again, I found myself picking him up and tucking him under my arm, but not as before to subdue him but this time to rescue him. He offered not the slightest resistance; it was if he knew why I was there and what I was doing. In no time at all I was clambering up the grassy bank out of the canal across the field and finally back at the lake where, with aching arms and a little out of breath, I gently popped him down by the water's edge. He ruffled his feathers and gave off a couple loud honks as if to say, 'I'm back dear, where are you?' His call was returned as his mate came gliding in from the far side of the lake to greet him where they entwined their long slender necks followed by a ritual of mutual preening. Ann and I continued to return to the lake but over time our visits became less frequent until one day they were gone.

We can only hope that they had a happy and long life together, they enriched our lives by their presence and will never be forgotten, particularly him with his belligerent, often amusing and sometimes downright painful antics!! And if you ever read this Mr D. Cooling (*I'm sure you will recognise the name*) I made the right choice!!!

It was around 10.30 am and I had just wandered across from the Wirral Country Park Visitor Centre to the Rehab Unit to check on a very sick seagull suffering from avian botulism. (*Botulism is a paralytic and often fatal condition particularly of fish-eating birds.*) The Unit had gained somewhat of a reputation with regards to the success rate in treating and rehabilitating birds suffering from the condition with one particular patient being a classic example as to how, with the correct treatment and process of rehabilitation, an animal can return to the wild to live a full and healthy life once again. The patient in question was a very sick young herring gull. It arrived as often creatures did wrapped in a jacket after being found by a dog walker on the beach. Its head was floppy with eyes reduced to tiny slits and beak open gasping for breath whilst emitting a foul smelling brown watery gunge from its backside. To all intents and purposes, it was dying! But like many creatures we gave it the benefit of the doubt and popped it into a hospital cage to rest.

To have attempted to administer fluids or food at this point would have tipped it over the edge, if it survived the night, we would then reassess the situation. The following morning, I removed the blanket I had draped over the cage fully expecting to find it as dead as a dodo but to my surprise it was still hanging on. As the days past it gradually found the strength to drink from a bowl soon followed by small amounts of food and very slowly but surely it got a little stronger until at last it could stand without falling over, its eyes opened, and its poo returned to its normal healthy black colour. After a few weeks of careful nursing, it was finally strong enough to be transferred into the seabird aviary allowing it to bathe and preen in order for its feathers to become watertight once again plus having ample room to exercise and fly around to build up lost muscle.

Some five weeks later it was given a British Trust for Ornithology leg ring and taken down to the old boat slipway on the beach at Thurstaston. The tide was on the ebb draining the deep muddy gullies as it slowly receded revealing more of the slipways stony and seaweed encrusted surface. I wandered out quite a way before placing the cardboard pet carrier on the still wet ground. It rocked from side to side a little as its occupant became restless seeming to sense that freedom was but a few moments away. I carefully opened the box and stood back a little: slowly but surely the gull came out and looked around for a minute or two before rapidly flapping its wings to lift it a foot or so off the ground before landing again. This went on for some time until finally it took off. Up and up, it went eventually to circle around a few times as if to get its bearings, occasionally almost hovering in the sky as it paused to shake its feathers before continuing on its journey of newfound freedom. And that was that another creature had beaten the odds to recover and return to the wild once more. But that wasn't the end of the story! Some five years later I received notification from the BTO that during a netting exercise to temporarily capture, record and ring sea birds, they had netted an adult herring gull wearing a leg ring with a number corresponding to a bird I had released some years previous and upon checking my records I discovered that it was the very same gull that had arrived at the Unit extremely poorly and a hairs breadth away from death!

Wildlife rehabilitation doesn't get any better than that!!

Another bird to arrive in a cardboard box, albeit a much bigger one and not by a member of the public this time but by the Merseyside Police Wildlife Crime Officer Andy McWilliam was a raven.

It had been taken from the wild as a youngster for the sole purpose of being used illegally as a decoy bird *(call bird)* in a Larson trap. (*A device used to trap wild birds mainly members of the corvid family, crows, magpies etc. where a bird is kept in a separate compartment as a decoy to attract others into the trap. At the time of writing, it can only be used legally under licence to trap Crows, Magpies, Rooks, Jackdaws and Jays. The trap was invented by a Danish gamekeeper by the name of Larson in the 1950's and is now banned in Denmark and viewed as cruel.*)

Thankfully, it was discovered and confiscated but not before taking its toll on the bird's condition and wellbeing. It was underweight, its feathers were dull and broken, it had lost two toes and due to muscle wastage couldn't fly, but despite its poor condition it was still an impressive bird. Ravens are the largest of the corvid family and can weigh up to 2 kg with a four-foot wingspan, they are also very intelligent and long lived. After a period of being on a decent diet its dull black plumage began to regain its gloss, its eyes became brighter, and it also became clear that due to being taken from the wild at such a young age, it was quite tame. Obviously, this made handling much easier but could put a big question mark over its suitability for rehabilitation. Once fit enough he was moved into a very large aviary which gave him plenty of room to exercise his wings to build up wasted muscle plus it would, over a period of time, give us the opportunity to assess his suitability for possible rehabilitation.

Within a few weeks he was flying around the aviary and looking good. But despite having regained weight and muscle we had our doubts about his ability ever to be able to fully fly well enough to survive in the wild plus the fact that he was also far too tame to be a true candidate for successful rehabilitation. Obviously with so many creatures around the place Ann and I would pass by his aviary umpteen times a day. It wasn't long before he got into the habit of flying down onto a low branch by the aviary wire knowing that we would pause for a while to spend the time of day with him.

He would shuffle along the perch until reaching the wire where, with his head cocked to one side he would make throaty rumbling sounds whereupon we would return the greeting with 'Hello' but Ann decided to take it a step further and rather than a simple 'Hello' would do a rather posh Leslie Phillips 'Hellooooo' and in no time at all our raven became quite the mimic with his very lifelike 'Helloooooos'. His reward for his endeavours would be a 'Good Boy' which, bless him, he tried his very best to mimic but he could never quite master the B's so rather than 'Good Boy' we got a 'Good Goy'!

He became so adept at his mimicry that he fooled quite a few visitors who, until proved otherwise, believed that somebody or other was playing tricks on them. Eventually as a permanent resident we decided he should have a name and decided on 'Bran' as the raven was the totem of the Welsh God, Bran the Blessed in Celtic mythology.

Another permanent resident once again came via Andy when he asked if I could assist on a warrant raid at an address in Liverpool. Apparently, someone had reported to the police that a neighbour was keeping a large bird of prey tethered in his back garden and was telling everyone that it was a honey buzzard taken from the wild. The honey buzzard (*Pernis apivorus*) is a rare summer visitor to the UK spending the winter in tropical Africa with their main food source being the insect larvae of wasps and bees but will also take small mammals, reptiles, eggs, and worms etc.

They are strictly protected under Schedule 1 of the Wildlife and Countryside Act 1981, and as such to get a tip off that one was being kept on a council estate in Liverpool created a bit of interest to say the least hence a warrant being issued to search the premises and yours truly being asked to attend. A few days later Andy and I, armed with the warrant, paid a visit to the property. Curtains twitched as neighbours peeked from behind curious as to why a police car was parked outside number 21 and what the burly copper and the short guy in a ranger uniform wanted of the occupier.

After a few bangs on the door an unshaven middle-aged bloke with straggly unkempt hair and clad in a stained light grey hoody top appeared. The sleeves of his top were rolled up to reveal faded tattoos whilst letters etched into his fingers in blue ink spelled out love and hate. On his lower torso he wore matching tracksuit bottoms tucked into white socks whilst in total contradiction to the rest of his typical scouse scally mode of dress, on his feet, rather than the obligatory Nike trainers he sported a tatty pair of grandad style grey chequered slippers. Andy proceeded to explain to the gentleman (*I use the term loosely!*) why we were there and that we had a warrant to search the premises.

A few expletives later, voiced in his best guttural scouse, he decided that rather than have the full force of the law descend upon him he would comply with the request. Whereupon he proceeded to lead us through the house down a narrow corridor by an uncarpeted staircase, past an open living room door, from where a very large top of the range television blasted out on full volume as half a dozen kids with runny noses watched *'Percy the Park Keeper and his Animals'* whilst feasting on jam butties. Quite in keeping I thought!! (*The film not the jam butties!*) Anyway, off we went past the living room and into a small, cluttered kitchen, the sink piled high with an assortment of pots and pans waiting to be washed whilst on a worktop an empty tin of baked beans streaked with tomato sauce sat amongst unwashed plates and a collection of half empty mugs of cold tea.

Our host was still complaining and cursing as he wrenched open the back kitchen door to scrape across the cracked and curled green lino to reveal a long narrow grassed back garden bordered on three sides by a tall panel fence.

To our right was a small wooden garden shed and running the full length of the garden parallel with the fence was a rope raised about a metre high and attached to wooden stakes at either end with a large brass ring threaded through it. A couple of the fence panels were heavily splattered with streaks of white and black bird poo indicating that the contraption and the suspected honey buzzard were connected.

When asked where the bird was, he replied, 'It's in there,' pointing to a small windowless shed.

Now normally this would be my cue to pull on my falconer's leather gauntlet and carefully enter the shed to retrieve the bird, but he would have none of it and insisted on bringing it out himself.

Amidst more cursing he vanished through the open back door to return with a very stained and cracked leather gauntlet only to disappear again into the shed. Various nonprintable expletives were emitted from within along with bumps and bangs and the flapping of wings before he reappeared with a large panting bird of prey uneasily gripping his now gloved hand and forearm. The bird was wearing falconer's anklets and jesses. A large brass swivel was attached to the lower section of the jesses with a blue thick nylon leash threaded through the bottom ring of the swivel. In the falconer's world this paraphernalia is known as furniture and is used to hold the bird on the fist, arm or be tethered to a bow perch or block.

It was immediately obvious that the bird wasn't a honey buzzard at all but a common buzzard *Buteo buteo* but nonetheless still afforded protection under the Wildlife and Countryside Act 1981 and as this bird wasn't wearing a closed leg ring nor microchipped, both of which would have led one to believe that it was captive bred and therefore legal, it was assumed to be wild bred and being kept illegally.

During questioning the guy admitted, as he put it in inverted commas, to have having found it in the wild. He also explained that it would often be attached by its leash to the large brass ring on the rope in order that it could fly along the length of the garden he also went on to say that on occasions it had attempted to fly over the garden fence only to come to a sudden stop as it came to the end of its leash, and much to his neighbour's alarm, discovered dangling upside down on the other side! Apparently, the reason for it being confined to the shed when we arrived.

The bird was immediately confiscated and taken to the Wildlife Rehab Unit to be cared for and to assess its suitability for possible rehabilitation. Due to its relatively small size and weight, I determined that it was a male, as in many birds of prey the male is the smaller of the sexes. It also soon became quite obvious that it must have been taken from the wild at a fairly young age due to its apparent tameness, albeit timid and nervous due to being kept in stressful conditions and poorly handled. But with patience and careful handling he began to settle down and we christened him Bert. Don't ask me why but it seemed a good idea at the time!

Eventually the guy was prosecuted, and the bird officially confiscated which meant that I could now begin to seriously work on him and as such began to train him to fly to the fist. Firstly, to assess his suitability for a possible gradual release and secondly for his own wellbeing and fitness, the idea being that the fitter he got and the more he was flown his natural hunting instincts would develop and his dependence on humans would decline, making him a suitable candidate for a soft release. (*A soft release is when a bird or animal is allowed to come and go at will from an enclosure where food is provided until the creature is proficient at catching natural prey and becomes self-sufficient.*) If done correctly this is a very effective and successful method of returning animals to the wild.

Unfortunately for Bert he failed the suitability assessment for a soft release due to his tameness but did eventually pass the fitness and wellbeing bit with flying colours. He could hunt to a certain degree, but buzzards tend to be lazy birds anyway much preferring an easy meal rather than an energy sapping chase. They are opportunistic predators taking a wide range of prey from small mammals to young rabbits but carrion in the form of a dead adult rabbit or whatever is much easier as are worms and frogs.

One summer evening I had taken Bert to a large rough field that I often used for training. The routine being that I would take him to the farthest end and sit him on a fence post. There he would sit watching me intently until I walked all the way back to the other end where, in eager anticipation, he would await my call for him to fly to my fist and receive his reward. Eventually with Bert at one end of the field and me at the other I would turn to face him whereupon he would lean forward ready for take off and as I raised my gloved hand and whistled, he would immediately take to the air, his wings flapping lazily just enough to keep him a couple of metres above the ground. As he got closer, he would glide silently on his large broad wings to drop a little lower to the ground until once more and with a few lazy wing beats would rise up to land on my gloved hand his talons gripping into the leather as he pulled at his reward. But this time was different! As he headed towards me it was obvious that I wasn't the main focus of his attention as his head moved from left to right scanning the rough grass below him. Suddenly and with lightning speed he swooped to the left and with talons outstretched hit the ground with a thump. I watched for a moment or two before wandering over to discover him devouring a frog!

Time moved on and Bert became a well-established permanent resident of the Rehabilitation Unit along with Bran the raven, Hamish the Scottish wildcat and of course the swans and foxes, spending his days in his large aviary or sitting on his bow perch in the garden. But one day I entered the aviary to take him out for a flight and much to my surprise I spotted a large dull white egg speckled with brown spots sitting in the grass. He had laid an egg!! Obviously, Bert had morphed into Bertina leaving my expertise in sexing the common buzzard very much a matter of opinion!!!

4

Time To Hang Up My Boots & A Few Escapades With Badger Diggers

With my foxes Muffles and Velvet now gone, and thankfully not the way Roger the Codger envisaged but naturally after having lived long lives along with Hamish the Scottish wildcat who eventually passed away in his native Scotland after having joined a captive breeding scheme, coupled with the official demise of the Unit I began to seriously ponder over how long I would have to go before I could hang up my boots and retire. I felt that I had achieved all I could with regards to managing the Wirral Ranger Service. The budgets were now in the green and the country parks were annually retaining the Green Flag awards.

But I was tiring of the mundane tasks of juggling budgets, applying for grants to keep heads above water not to mention the unpleasant task of occasionally having to officially discipline a wayward member of staff which of course involved liaising with union reps and the council's Human Resources department plus the seemingly never-ending list of meetings. As Head Ranger I would chair the monthly senior ranger meetings as well as attending council management meetings, directors' meetings, auditors' meetings, and last but not least accountant meetings. I've always been of the opinion that if you are having a meeting it should be for a good reason, with the positive outcome of benefitting the service and the authority, not merely to sit round a table drinking coffee whilst flitting from one agenda topic to the next just to tick a box and say we've had a meeting. Or one that goes aimlessly round in circles so many times that it eventually becomes in danger of vanishing up its own orifice, or for someone to relish the sound of their own voice for so long that heads begin to droop with only the occasional snore to break the monotony.

Unfortunately, the vast majority of meetings tended to be of the latter but of course it goes without saying that the senior ranger meetings were obviously the exception to the rule and were absolutely brimming with positivity and good-hearted banter! (*I should have been so lucky!*)

Another laborious task was having to tolerate the daily negativity towards the ranger service from the Head of Parks and Open Spaces, the infamous D. Cooling. I can only imagine that it stemmed from some years previous when someone in their misguided wisdom decided that he should be promoted from a pen pusher, hidden away in some far distant cobwebbed corner of the council, to Principal Officer overseeing the management of the ranger service. Unfortunately for him he quickly discovered that his non-existent people management skills combined with his total lack of knowledge and overtly obvious disinterest in anything remotely connected to conservation didn't exactly do an awful lot to gain him the trust and respect of his staff. Not to mention his egotistical attitude which served only to exasperate them even further and boy did they show it!

His mere presence was like a red rag to a bull, and they took great delight in winding him up. One damp rainy morning and sporting a pair of brand new bright green Hunter wellies he was making his way along the wooden bridge over the large pond towards the Wirral Country Park Visitor Centre to chair one of his monthly ranger staff meetings. Now the wellies were ok for keeping one's feet dry but didn't provide the greatest grip in the world on a wet slippery surface and as he briskly marched towards the main entrance, observed by his little band of rebellious rangers, his bright green wellies relinquished their tenuous grip on terra firma and amidst roars of uncontrollable laughter and with splaying arms and legs he hit the deck!! And to make matters worse the rangers, of which I was one in those far off days, took the bit in their teeth and turned the meeting into a shambles leaving him red faced and furious.

Ironically it was Roger C. that, during one of our more civil conversations, I happened to mention that I was thinking of applying for early retirement. A week later as I was walking past his office, he called me in and asked if I had gone any further with my thoughts of retiring. I told him that I hadn't and to my surprise asked me to close the door whereupon he advised me not to pursue it as he had heard a whisper that the council were about to invite staff to apply for EVR *(early voluntary retirement)* which of course would include an enhanced financial package. It was good of him to give me the heads up, but I couldn't help but be pessimistic and wonder if he had an ulterior motive. After all, with the Head Ranger post vacant it would leave the door wide open for another cost cutting exercise.

A week later a standard letter popped through the post explaining the terms of the package and that applications had to be in by a certain date. It also explained that the offer would run for a limited term of four weeks and that applicants would be notified one way or the other within that time frame. Needless to say, I applied and with eager anticipation awaited the outcome. Week one went by followed by week two and three and still no confirmation one way or the other. I spoke to people in HQ who had applied around the same time as me and yes, they had received a letter informing them of the result. Some ecstatic that they were off down the flowery road to retirement and freedom with a few quid in their pockets whilst others were despondent at the thought of spending another few years segregated to their partitioned little cubicle in HQ's large open plan office, tapping away at a grubby crumb encrusted computer keyboard. Others within park maintenance shuddered at the thought of even more years of riding around on a sit on mower cutting roadside grass verges, blue plastic ear defenders dulling the sound of the engine and the constant stream of passing traffic belching out their choking exhaust fumes. And to my surprise I learned that even Rodger the Codger had applied and been informed of his success. Apparently, he was spotted doing a jig in his office celebrating the thought of escaping from HQ and the apron strings of his master.

But what of me? Had my application been lost in the system? Wednesday of week four arrived and still no news, another two days and that was it, I wouldn't be going anywhere and as such decided that it was time to start asking questions.

My first port of call was the personnel department who informed me that yes, they had received my application but were awaiting a response from J.L. the director of Wirral's Leisure Service which the Parks and Open Spaces department fell under. I had known him for many years and always regarded him as a decent sort of chap and as such wasted no time in contacting him. I explained my predicament along with my overwhelming desire to wave farewell to the council. He listened intently but without much comment until eventually he promised to look into it. On the final day and with only a couple of hours to spare I received notification that my application had been accepted! It was so close to the wire that personnel had to email me the conformation rather than posting out the standard letter. Talk about making me sweat!!!

A few days later after spending the morning doing my rounds visiting the various country parks and catching up with staff I decided to wander into HQ and catch up on paperwork that was by now beginning to resemble a wobbly skyscraper rising up from my in-tray with the slightest whiff of a breeze or vibration from passing feet sending an avalanche of A4 sheets of memos and minutes and agendas from numerous meetings to come tumbling down to land in a disordered mess on my desktop.

After the usual battle to find a vacant parking place I made my way to reception and after scanning my pass to gain entry, I entered the inner sanctum of Westminster House, Wirral Council's Leisure Services HQ. Rather than take the lift I briskly climbed the stairs to the third floor and proceeded down the corridor to pass by the open doored drab little offices of D.C. and R.C. Yes, I know they sound like an alternative electric current but these two may have had a reputation for being a couple of bright sparks but sadly for all the wrong reasons! Eventually I entered the large open plan office with its lines of screened off little blue fabric cubicles each furnished with a light oak coloured laminated desk standing upon grey metal legs. A forlorn looking house plant sat atop of a grey filing cabinet its leaves drooping and tinged with brown as it slowly croaked of thirst whilst the staff perched upon their blue fabric swivel chairs tapped away on their crumb encrusted computer keyboards.

I was just about to plonk myself down at my desk when J.L. appeared and asked if I wouldn't mind wandering down to his office for a chat. A few minutes later I was knocking on his secretary's door and as I entered was quickly ushered through a second door into a spacious bright room furnished with posh looking black vinyl leatherette chairs spread around a long light oak veneered executive meeting table. Various large, framed prints depicting Wirral's coastal views adorned the walls whilst brightly coloured flowers in sparkling glass vases sat upon the table and bookshelves. What a contrast to the dingy offices of D.C. and R.C. and the thirsty drooping plants of the open plan office floor!

He shook my hand and in his soft Scottish lilt invited me to sit down whilst he organised coffee and ask his secretary to hold his calls. After a minute or two he returned to sit opposite, and we chatted about this and that as the aroma of freshly brewed ground coffee wafted from the adjoining office. Eventually our general chit chat was interrupted by the arrival of that delicious smelling brew along with a floral decorated plate of digestive biscuits coated in dark chocolate. Whilst sipping coffee and nibbling on digestives he finally came down to the reason for our informal chat by saying that he was sorry for delaying the response to my application for early retirement followed by explaining that various departments, including the ranger service, were being considered for privatisation. I had heard whispers to that effect but nothing concrete and, unbeknownst to me, if privatisation came to fruition it was hoped that I would be the one to oversee the transition from an authority run ranger service to a private one and from then on to act as middle-man between the two. I promptly told him that I couldn't think of anything worse and shuddered at the prospect of spending my final working years as a pen pusher and mediator.

He said that he fully understood and respected my views and with coffee downed and digestives devoured we parted on good terms, and I returned to my desk.

And so it came to pass that on the 31st December 2010 my 28 years of employment within the Wirral Ranger Service officially ended and I was no longer a ranger. I had strived long and hard to get a foothold on the very first rungs of that long shaky ladder where, if you were lucky, it just might lead to a full-time ranger post. I had studied the ins and outs of wildlife conservation, habitat, and woodland management, been on just about every course imaginable from first aid to public speaking and during my early days with Lancashire County Council Ranger Service passed numerous practical assessments in navigation and fell rescue. But all that was many moons ago and now 35 years on from my very first inaugural days with L.C.C., it had turned full circle. I had achieved my ambition to become not only a ranger but Head Ranger and Wildlife Officer and to say that my career had been unusual would be an understatement!

I had been a ranger in the full sense of the word but also cared for, and rehabilitated, many different species of wildlife from peregrine falcons to badgers, seals, stoats and weasels to name but a tiny few. I had been involved in the making of wildlife related television programmes, met, and worked alongside a few famous characters, written papers on wildlife care and rehabilitation and lectured far and wide on the subject. But now it was over! It was time to take stock and for my wife Ann and I to decide on our future whatever that may be. Our first consideration was where to live.

For the past 28 years we had resided in the council owned detached three bedroomed house known as 2 Rangers Cottage at Wirral Country Park, Thurstaston. Initially it came with the job, but it was now no longer a tied property meaning that we could, if we so wished, continue to rent it, or even buy it. It was all a lot to take in and as such decided to mull things over for a while before making a final decision. It was quite poignant really in that in September 1982 when I attended the interview for the post of Countryside Ranger at Wirral Country Park, I had heard a whisper that 2 Rangers Cottage had just become vacant and towards the end of the interview when the question was asked, "Well Mr Ingham, do you have any questions?"

Armed in the knowledge that they were interviewing for two ranger posts and with only one vacant cottage I made it quite clear that if offered a post I would only accept if they also offered the cottage, which of course they did otherwise I wouldn't be sat here writing this. And now here we were some 28 years later trying to decide whether to stay or move. As you can imagine after living there for such a long time the place held a multitude of memories particularly of our whippets, Sally, Tigger, Brock and little Eric, the Italian greyhound who could sniff out a discarded butty in a dense clump of heather half a mile away! The goats Candy, Polly, Tansy, Jasmine, and Winkle plus Guy the pony. Badgers Toby, Pickles, Cassie, Kippy, Millie and Basil, Hamish the Scottish wildcat, foxes Muffles and Velvet and of course the swans!! Sadly, all now gone but not forgotten. They still live on, not just in memories but also in photographs and of course my writings, with some being the basis of characters in my children's book, *The Tales of Old Billy Badger*.

Memories not only of wildlife but also of people, places, and events and of television crews and a few well-known faces. The ranger service published a quarterly Wirral Countryside Newsletter brimming with articles and of up-and-coming events. I usually submitted an article or two on the latest happenings at the Wildlife Rehab Unit some of which I recently came across dated from 1984 to 1994 stored away in a dusty cardboard box hiding away on a shelf in my study and I couldn't resist but to sift through them. It's amazing how an old, cobwebbed corner of the brain can be dusted off and revitalised to bring back memories as if it was yesterday!

To read of the activities put on by the ranger service all those years ago and of rangers whose names long since forgotten in the mists of time suddenly came flooding back. To read my own articles written all those years ago with titles such as 'Seal of Approval,' 'The Bridgemere Badgers,' 'Barn Owl Breeding & Release,' 'Our Much Maligned Urban Fox,' 'From Suez to the Dee,' 'Deer Hunting in Birkenhead' and 'Nigel the Nighthawk,' all brought back vivid memories of those events. In the spring of 1994, I wrote an article entitled 'Extracts from the Wildlife Rehabilitation Unit's Diary,' noting such events as on the 4th Jan. '94 at 3 pm a sparrow hawk was brought in by the RSPCA. I noted no visible injuries, in good bodily condition, appears concussed, treat for shock. 5th Jan. much brighter, placed in aviary, flying well, released 1pm, weather fine & mild. On the 23rd Jan., a heron was handed in, small wound to left side of chest, possibly caused by airgun pellet, very thin and weak. Probably a combination of the wound and the recent freezing weather conditions. Treat for shock, i.e. warmth and rest. X-ray showed no internal damage or lead shot, tube fed liquid followed by gentle force feeding. 24th Jan. taking fish from the hand. 27th Jan. feeding on its own. 30th Jan. much stronger and placed in large aviary, 25th Jan. feeding and flying well. Awaiting for the weather to improve before release.

Other entries include a long-eared owl on the 1st Feb. A tawny owl on the 23rd Feb. and a fox on the 24th Feb. and so on. Stored alongside the newsletters were various journals featuring articles about the work of the Wildlife Rehab Unit written either by myself or a journalist. There was a 1987 RSPCA magazine featuring a full-page article by RSPCA Inspector Barry Williams telling the tale of him bringing a badger cub to the Unit and its eventual successful rehabilitation along with other rescued cubs.

Anyone having read *From Badgers to Nighthawks* may remember the story of the hand rearing of the five badger cubs, Toby, Pickles, Milly, Kippy and Cassie and their eventual return to the wild followed by their many adventures living as wild creatures told in chapters six and seven. Cassie was the cub rescued by Barry. She was found curled up next to a dead sheep, cold and underweight and infested with fleas and lice but she made a full recovery and eventually lived the life of a truly wild badger. Other journals included a Jan 1991 issue of 'Veterinary Nursing' the journal for The British Veterinary Nursing Association featuring a technical paper I had written on the housing, care, and treatment of wildlife within a Veterinary Surgery environment plus lengthy feature articles in the January 1992, January 1994, and February 1998 issues of 'Cheshire Life'.

I was once even featured in 'Hello' magazine! Unfortunately for all the wrong reasons as they had published quite an extensive article on a massive oil spill in the Mersey Estuary originating from Shell UK's Refinery in Ellesmere Port. Inevitably I became involved in the treatment of many casualties from gulls, gannets, ducks, waders, and herons to name but a sad few. They had included a picture of me holding a dead cormorant that looked more like a large black solidified lump of oil than what had once been a living creature. Unfortunately, at that time the cleaning and rehabilitation of victims of pollution, particularly from oil spills was still very much a hit and miss affair *(and unfortunately still is despite the improvements in knowledge, facilities, and medication)* with many dying of shock, stress or ingesting the pollutant by attempting to clean themselves. Even if we were successful in removing every trace of oil from the body and feathers many would still succumb, sometimes as long as a few weeks later from internal problems. In a captive environment a cleaned bird may seem absolutely fine, swimming, diving and eating well but once faced with the trials and tribulations of the wild, particularly at sea, any weakness in bodily condition or water tightness of the plumage would quickly prove fatal.

The spill made international news with television crews from a host of broadcasting companies not only on the scene but also at the Wildlife Rehab Unit with me being asked constantly on my thoughts of the disaster. I found this particularly frustrating in that my first priority was to try and help these poor stricken creatures that were arriving via RSPCA vehicles and not to waste time talking into a microphone, but people needed to see for themselves what a catastrophic disaster it was and the only way that could be done was through the media of television.

But that was in the past, time had moved on bringing with it other unforgettable events some sad, some exhilarating and some amusing. One such event was the time I got a call from an off-duty police officer who had a pathological hatred of badger diggers *(don't we all!!)* informing me that a gang of known diggers armed with spades and dogs were walking through West Kirby in the direction of Wirral Country Park and could I assist. I set off in my canvas topped short, wheeled base green Land Rover emblazed with its yellow and green Countryside Ranger sign informing all and sundry that it wasn't being driven by a mere mortal.

We had arranged to meet up, me in the Landy and he in his own car in the direction they were last reported and as I was driving up Banks Road the officer, a PC Vaughan, was approaching in the opposite direction when lo and behold who should be in his sights but the badger diggers.

He put his foot down hard on the accelerator and when level with the gang slammed on the brakes to screech to a halt with the driver's door almost parting from its hinges as he leapt out like an SAS warrior on steroids to bundle the scum bags into a disused shop doorway with me arriving on the scene literally minutes later.

Now this of course was before the advent of mobile phones, and as I jumped out of the Landy to help and before I could utter a word he said, "Hold them there Malcolm, whilst I nip into the pub across the road to call the station for back-up."

Before I could say boo to a goose, I was on my little own with five perspiring Neanderthal looking thugs still reeling from the screaming, shouting madman that had propelled himself from a car to, within seconds, have them all huddled like lambs in a doorway.

Amidst all the unprintable expletives and screams of we know he's a copper, he can't do this we're going to report him all I could think of was that any minute now they are going to do a runner and there wasn't a thing I could do to stop them. I envisaged them taking off like a herd of hairy cattle trampling me into the ground in the process. PC Vaughan couldn't have been away more than five minutes, but it seemed an age as I bluffed my way through with a bit of false bravado! But it must have worked as they didn't do a runner and stayed put until back up arrived in the form a blue and white panda police car.

Another incident involving PC Vaughan *(to be honest there were quite a few!)* happened one evening whilst I was sat at home watching telly when the telephone rang and upon picking up the receiver I heard his gruff voice saying, "Malcolm, just had a report of a dodgy looking car parked up by Thurstaston church fancy checking it out?"

Needless to say, off I went culminating with the two of us, after determining that the vehicle was empty, inspecting it from top to bottom by torchlight. A dog cage sat in the back, straw, along with discarded cigarette packets lay scattered around the floor, and for all the world it fit the bill of a digger's vehicle. (*it's quite common for diggers to hunt badger with dogs and high*-powered *torch beam after dark in the hope of catching them above ground and set the dogs on them)*. We decided that the owners of the vehicle could be anywhere it and would be futile to go looking for them. Even if we were to spot the high-powered beam of their lamping torch the chances of catching them were slim. Once the light went out, they would merely vanish once again into the night. We decided that the best course of action would be to hide in the shadows and wait for them to return but just in case they decided to speed off before we could get to them, we let the tyres down.

Within minutes the sound of hissing air escaping from tyre valves broke the silence of the night and with tyres as flat as a pancake we laid in wait. Thirty minutes went by with no sign of a soul and then we saw movement. Our hearts began to race with anticipation, the adrenalin began to pump, and we were like two concealed lions ready to pounce on prey. And then it happened! A lone figure appeared out of the shadows to approach the vehicle but there was something amiss. This wasn't a burly unshaven heavily tattooed badger digger, at least not unless they were now taking their grandads out to participate in their sick pastimes.

Finally, the figure reached the vehicle and with a shaky hand inserted the key to unlock the driver's door. We looked at each other with horror and disbelief! Surely, it's not his car, he doesn't even have a dog we whispered as we broke cover to reveal ourselves, firstly to stop him from attempting to drive off with flat tyres, secondly to eat humble pie and thirdly, to pump the blooming tyres back up again. Thankfully once we explained who we were and why we had vandalised his car he was extraordinarily understanding about it all. He had in fact been visiting a friend who lived in a cottage down a nearby pot holed track and didn't fancy taking the car down in the dark hence leaving it by the church.

Whilst we are on the subject of PC Vaughan I may as well relate a few more of his exploits. It was a Thursday afternoon, just turned mid-day and I was heading along the A540 towards Heswall when my radio crackled into life informing me that a vehicle containing known badger diggers had been seen stationary at the traffic lights in Heswall heading along the A540 towards West Kirby and that the police were on route from Hoylake Police Station. Some ten minutes later I was passing through those very same lights when about a mile farther on I spotted two police cars parked up in a lay by with flashing blue lights and as I got closer I could see that they had pulled the car over and that an officer was talking to the occupants through the wound down driver's window, whilst a second was giving the vehicle the once over and checking the contents of the boot. As

I pulled in to the lay by, I could see a third officer under the raised bonnet of the car which I thought a little strange.

As I got out he sauntered over and yes, you have guessed it, it was PC Vaughan who went on to explain that the car was legal and nothing untoward had been found and as such could find no reason to detain the occupants or the vehicle and they had been strongly advised to get themselves back to Liverpool asap and not bother to return.

Curious as to why PC Vaughan should have been under the bonnet I put the question to him and with a wink and a wry smile he whispered, "I've swapped the plug leads over!!" Whereupon he ordered them to move on and after a few unsuccessful attempts to comply and with the battery beginning to drain, the car finally burst into life and off they went albeit rather slowly amidst a fair amount of bouncing and backfiring!

I could reminisce for evermore about the tricks we got up to whilst in pursuit of badger diggers and baiters but on the pretext of not wishing to incriminate myself I shall refrain from going into too much detail with regards to some. Needless to say, we played dirty! But I will relate one or two incidents that were not directly instigated by myself or involved PC Vaughan.

For those of you reading this who are not fully familiar with the type of person who participates in badger digging and baiting or, for that matter, any other illegal and barbaric blood sport, they are generally as thick as two short planks, have a blood lust for cruelty, are aggressive bullies and above all else absolute cowards!

Every Friday night I would get a tip off via telephone from Kenny M. a train driver on the Liverpool to Wirral run that a gang had boarded the train in Liverpool fully equipped to spend the night lamping badger i.e.- lurcher type dogs, powerful battery powered lights and often a 12-bore shotgun. I won't elaborate too much due to the barbaric nature of the hunt but in a nutshell, they would catch a badger in the beam of the powerful light beam and release the dogs to pursue it.

We had tried everything possible to try and catch them, but it proved impossible for as soon as they left the station at Hooton, they vanished into the night only to reappear again the following morning to catch the first train back to Liverpool. It was pointless trying to apprehend them at the station due to having no proof as to what they had been up to - they had to be caught in the act. The council at that time had recruited a small team of individuals who, rather loosely, went under the title of Park Police. They had no powers of arrest and were, to all intents and purposes, security personnel. They were an interesting bunch of individuals from an eclectic mix of backgrounds with some, when not in work, moonlighting as bouncers, *(sorry, doormen)* or similar part time occupations that required a certain type of person. To say that they were a hot-headed bunch would be an understatement and they led their manager a merry dance who, despite being a decent sort of chap, was unfortunately way out of his comfort zone when it came to managing such an unruly bunch of characters. Anyway, despite their failings, at least from official point of view, they were a godsend to me!

Occasionally Ann and I would socialise with them and their wives and partners *(plenty of booze and usually ending up a bit unruly!)* and on one occasion I just happened to mention the ongoing problem with these guys from Liverpool and before I knew it a plan was hatched!

To cut a long story short the idea was that a few of them, obviously out of uniform, would form a reception party for the Liverpool mob in an effort to explain to them the error of their ways and that it would be much appreciated and healthier for them if they would desist from coming over to Wirral to harass our little black and white badger friends.

We decided on a dummy run with the control centre being our living room awaiting the call from Kenny M. that they were on their way. Once received, I would radio through that it was game on. All radios were to be left open enabling everyone involved to hear the various conversations etc. It was a near disaster! Our guys were on their way to the railway station in a beat-up transit van when the police pulled them over for a routine check. Luckily, the van was legal, but they still got a grilling as to where they were going and what for at such a late hour. Thankfully, they talked their way out of it and aborted the exercise. But after a debrief and a few minor modifications we decided on the real thing and this time it went like clockwork!

The call came from Kenny M., the radio call was made to the team and as the last train of the night pulled into the deserted railway station the radio crackled into life.

"You in position number two?"

"Affirmative number one."

"Number three here number one, the trains approaching."

"Copy that number three."

Slowly the train entered the station to come to a screeching, clunking halt as Kenny M. applied the brakes. The doors opened with the only passengers being the Liverpool gang and their dogs. First one, then a second then, a third, until all five had alighted. They paused on the platform for a minute or two to light cigarettes and untangle their dogs before, amidst much laughter and swearing, they headed for the exit that led them into the now empty, dimly lit car park. That is with the exception of an old nondescript brown transit van tucked away in a far shadowy corner.

As the rowdy gang made their way into the shadows the redness of their cigarettes burning bright in the darkness the radios crackled into life once again.

"Number two here, number one, heading your way."

"Copy that, ready and waiting!"

Next to come crackling through the radio was a jumble of punching sounds followed by grunts, groans, and barking dogs. It was all over in a matter of minutes! One of the team had been assigned to ensure that the dogs came to no harm and didn't run off into the night whilst the others joined in the fun. I received a call from Kenny M. the following day to inform me that in the early hours as he was taking an empty train through Hooton station back to Liverpool, the five battered and bruised badger hunters and their dogs were on the platform frantically waving their arms in a feeble attempt to hitch a ride back to Liverpool. Needless to say, Kenny M. waved them a goodbye kiss. The message seemingly got through as we didn't hear from them again.

Before I finally depart from my reminiscing, I must relate one more incident involving the council's Park Police which demonstrates the loyalty that had developed between us. I wasn't their boss and had no authority over them whatsoever but when it came down to the nitty gritty, they were there.

This incident involved not badger hunters but a burglar.

The Visitor Centre at Wirral Country Park, prior to being alarmed, had been broken into on two occasions in quick succession and a request was put to the manager of the Park Police for nightly patrols which was granted. Now, driving slowly around the car parks in a marked vehicle is one thing, but if the perpetrator is coming across the fields to carry out his dastardly deed he won't be seen. So, a plan was hatched. Three of the Park Police would hide in the Visitor Centre, one in my office, one in the darkness of the long corridor whilst a third would be in wait crouched behind the counter.

On the third night of the stake out the intruder decided that the time was ripe for another little excursion into the centre to see what was worth nicking this time. Obviously, things had been made quite easy for him and in no time at all he was in and by the light of his dimly lit torch made his way to the counter. All was silent and as far as he was concerned the place was his to ransack. He confidently lifted the hinged section of the countertop to pass behind and as he did so got an almighty smack on the kneecaps with a solid wooden baton. Apparently, he let out an ear-piercing scream of agony and shock as he crumpled to the floor.

Within minutes my home telephone was ringing to inform me that they had him in custody and could I make my way there. As I approached the centre over the wooden bridge spanning the pond the place was lit up like Blackpool illuminations.

As I entered, I enquired as to where he was with the reply being, "He's in there," pointing to my office. I opened the door to see an ashen faced burglar sat in a chair with the burly hands of two of the Park Police resting heavily on his shoulders.

Before I could utter a word, the team leader posed the question, "What do you want us to do with him Mal?" Followed by, "If you like we can give him a thumping, kick his backside across the bridge and dump him in the pond."

"Just say the word Mal and consider it done!"

The guy's face turned ashen as he began to visibly tremble with fear and blubber for clemency. I must admit that the appeal of prolonging his suffering was very tempting. I even considered playing along and giving the go ahead but upon reflection decided that even if I wasn't serious they probably were and I didn't fancy the prospect of hauling a soggy, weed laden, not to say battered and bruised burglar from the watery depths and, as such, decided that it would be wiser to play it by the book and hand him over to the local constabulary. To say that he welcomed the presence of a bona fide policeman with open arms would be an understatement!!

Reminiscing over past events and characters can be quite thought provoking and tends to stimulate the brain to dust away the cobwebs to evoke even more memories such as the time the park police rammed a badger diggers vehicle and caused what was officially a road traffic accident!

It all started one Saturday morning. I was off duty and probably doing something or other around the Rehab Unit when the telephone rang to say that known badger diggers were in the area and that one of my rangers was heading towards the scene. I grabbed my radio and accompanied by my wife Ann headed off in our car with the intention of meeting up with the ranger. We hadn't gone far when my radio crackled into life with the ranger informing me that the diggers were legging it at full pelt across a field in the direction of their vehicle which was parked by a roadside and that the park police were on their way.

A few minutes later the radio crackled into life again with a breathless and adrenalin pumped voice saying, "They have made it to their vehicle and are about to drive off and I can see two park police vans approaching."

What should we do? By this time and unbeknownst to me the Park Police were listening into the conversation. Ann, who, if at all possible, always insisted on accompanying me on these call outs and with a tendency to get a little carried away, screamed "Ram em!"

The radio crackled into life again with a "Could you repeat that?"

By this time, my adrenalin was also pumping and without considering the consequences shouted down the receiver "Stop 'em!" And stop 'em they did!!

I arrived on the scene to discover the digger's vehicle sandwiched between two park police vans with glass from shattered headlights littering the road and pavement and four very irate and blaspheming diggers lined up against a fence watched over by the ranger and four burly park police. As I climbed out of my vehicle, I recognised the familiar face of a motorcycle cop heading towards me, his high powered yellow and blue BMW motorcycle propped on its standby the roadside with blue flashing light indicating to passing motorists that a road traffic accident had taken place.

His first words were, "Blimey Malcolm, what the *bleep, bleep, bleep* happened here?"

I explained who the four crimson faced blaspheming individuals were but as far as the RTA was concerned, I was struggling to come up with a reasonable explanation. To cut a long story short he went through all the formal procedures for dealing with an RTA after which he ordered the diggers, whose only transgression had been to trespass, to get in their vehicle and get themselves back to Liverpool.

Thankfully, the vehicle was still roadworthy albeit minus a headlight and a couple of taillights and amidst more bouts of cursing and swearing they eventually headed off in the general direction of the Mersey Tunnel. After they had left, he took me to one side and sympathetically explained that he would see what he could do to smooth things over after which he gave the Park Police a lecture on the stupidity of their actions. They took it all in like sheepish naughty schoolboys in the headmaster's office knowing full well that if found in similar circumstances they would, in all probability, do it all over again! Don't ask me how but miraculously no action was taken, and it was all brushed under the carpet.

On a final note, the ranger in question had another altercation with one of the diggers known as Kelly a few months later whereupon he found himself spread eagled over the bonnet of Kelly's vehicle as it sped down the road in an attempt to escape. He eventually slid off to land in a heap on the pavement thankfully suffering nothing more serious than a few cuts and bruises. Kelly was later arrested with the case eventually going to Liverpool Crown Court. His defence was that having come across this ranger before he panicked hence putting his foot down hard on the accelerator when suddenly the ranger leapt onto the bonnet and with one hand gripping onto a wiper blade for support, hammered on the windscreen with the other before sliding off onto the pavement. Unbelievably a jury of twelve, who having been convinced by the defence that the ranger in question had capabilities that James Bond himself would have been proud of, fell hook line and sinker with Kelly's defence's version of events and found him not guilty of all charges.

He couldn't believe his luck and gleefully danced out of court yelling, "See you back on Wirral next week you ******* losers!!"

But we did have our successes with one being of particular note. It was around mid-afternoon when I got a call one day from a resident in West Kirby saying that two guys with spades and dogs were digging a known fox earth on scrubland directly opposite their bungalow and could I do something about it? I immediately rang the local police station who promised to send a constable to meet me at the scene, after which I made my way there.

Thankfully, the police car pulled up as I arrived whereupon the PC and I made our way down a potholed track to the scene. We immediately saw that extensive digging had taken place on a number of holes. A terrier dog was halfway down a hole, whilst others had been blocked with soil and turf. From the word go the diggers were very uncooperative and aggressive with one threatening me with a spade, whilst the other attempted to kick soil and turf into a hole despite being asked not to by the PC. They denied digging for fox insisting that they were merely rabbiting. They were also on council land not covered by bylaws and even if they had admitted being after fox, due to the fox not afforded legal protection, there was not a lot could have been done anyway. To cut a long story short the PC took their details and sent them on their way but I had my suspicions that they had indeed killed a fox and buried it and if that was the case they may have committed an offence under the new Wild Mammals (Protection) Act of 1996 which to quote - *makes provision for the protection of wild mammals from certain cruel acts by stating that any person who - mutilates, kicks, beats, nails or otherwise impale, stab, burn, stone, drown, crush or asphyxiate any wild mammal with intent to cause unnecessary suffering shall be guilty of an offence.*

Once the diggers had left the scene I began to remove the soil and turf that one of them had been kicking into one of the holes and soon retrieved the body of a fox which I took to a local vet for postmortem which revealed that the fox had suffered extensive injuries including lacerations to the liver plus having a substantial amount of soil in the mouth and oesophagus.

I approached the RSPCA with my evidence and postmortem report in the hope that they would consider a prosecution. Unfortunately, they declined due to the fact that a prosecution would be costly with a very slim chance of a successful outcome. However not to be put off I stored the body in a freezer in the hope that they would reconsider. Some months later the

RSPCA contacted me to request a second postmortem the results of which once again revealed a substantial amount of soil down the oesophagus. This categorically proved that it had in fact died from asphyxiation due to inhaling soil and other debris whilst being buried alive. The RSPCA finally took the prosecution and won! Both defendants were found guilty of causing intentional unnecessary suffering resulting in the death of a wild mammal contrary to the Wild Mammal (Protection) Act of 1996. I was informed at the time that it was the first successful prosecution under the act.

But all that was now nothing more than history, I was now officially retired and as far as I was concerned my days of confronting such people were over and done with, but little did, I know what the future had in store! But for now, at least, my mind was occupied with the practicalities of our immediate future, with the big question being, do we stay where we are or do we move on.

5

A Conspiracy Of Ravens & A New Beginning

The quandary on whether to stay or move on went on for some time as we weighed up the pros and cons. 2 Rangers Cottage held a lot of memories, not just of the multitude of creatures that had passed through the Wildlife Rehab Unit to eventually return to a life in the wild, but also of the ones that had been part and parcel of the place as permanent residents such as Muffles and Velvet and Basil the badger, not to mention the goats, chickens and dogs to name but a few that over the years had called the place their home. Sadly, now all gone and buried in and around the garden. The log cabin that, over the years, had seen a multitude of creatures pass through its door whilst serving as the hospital unit now lay empty and forlorn as did the fox's enclosures and the assortment of aviaries. But not all were empty, we still had (*Bert*) Bertina the buzzard and Bran the raven plus two ancient tawny owls and a barn owl.

After much deliberation we decided that a complete change was needed and as such began to explore the possibility of buying a place in North Wales. My work had taken me over the border into Denbighshire on many occasions either whilst assisting the Forestry Commission with barn owl conservation and reintroduction, rehabilitating a long-eared owl, or spending many months in the woods gradually returning a clan of orphaned young badgers back to the wild.

But not all of our explorations over the border were work orientated as it was also one of our favourite spots for rambling the hills of the Clwydian Range or the mountains of Eryri N.P. (*Snowdonia*) with Brock the whippet and Eric our Italian greyhound. For anyone not familiar with the breed, the Italian greyhound is more like a miniature whippet than a greyhound and despite Eric's diminutive stature and appearing rather delicate, he could tramp the hills with the best of them and as mentioned previous, had an uncanny knack of sniffing out a walker's discarded bacon butty half a mile away. He made a comical sight as he bounded through the heather in search of his prize. He would be there one minute and gone the next as the purple mass swallowed him up only for him to reappear again, tail wagging and head held aloft with the remains of a bacon butty in his mouth.

But one of the most unusual events whilst out walking the Clwydian hills happened as we were walking along a winding rough track, Brock walking alongside us with Eric a little way ahead when we heard the distinctive throaty *kraa-kraa* call of ravens as they circled overhead. As we were quite close to a woodland copse where a pair nested, we thought nothing of it. First there were two, but then three and then four until we had quite a flock of them flying around *(the collective noun for a flock of ravens is an unkindness or a conspiracy of ravens).* They circled above calling loudly until, to our utter surprise not to mention poor Eric's, they began to dive bomb him! They weren't actually making contact but were definitely swooping very low above him until Ann swooped him up and tucked him under her arm. This happened in the month of June and as ravens can breed anytime from late January to early May, juveniles or other non-breeding birds not holding territory can form flocks and I can only assume that was case with these birds and that they had possibly mistaken poor Eric for a predator, hence mobbing him.

But considering just how intelligent and playful ravens are perhaps they were just having fun. A couple of years prior to this at the same spot we observed a flock of cuckoos flying around in the vicinity of the woodland. Of course, cuckoos are solitary birds and not normally seen in flocks. *(The collective noun for a flock of cuckoos is an asylum of cuckoos).* After leaving the nest young cuckoos can form flocks prior to their migration to Africa towards the end of September. The adults, who having laid their egg in the nest of another bird, have no parental responsibilities to worry about and will often migrate back to Africa as early as June leaving their offspring to be cared for by its foster parent.

Anyway, as our search for a new home continued, we had to decide what we were going to do with Bertina and Bran, the buzzard and raven. Both were beyond redemption insofar as rehabilitation was concerned leaving them destined for a life of captivity. Quality of life is paramount for any creature in captivity and as such each would need a very large spacious aviary. Unfortunately, it was very unlikely that we would be able to afford to buy a place with enough land to allow us to give them the space they needed, so it was imperative that we found them new homes. Obviously, their future welfare was of utmost concern and whoever took them on would have to be knowledgeable with regards to caring for their species and be prepared to give them a good quality of life which obviously entailed having suitable accommodation.

We made numerous enquiries but for various reasons none were considered suitable until one day we were contacted by a lady from Yorkshire who boasted a doctorate degree in avian psychology with a particular interest in raptors and had a yearning to train a common buzzard to fly free. She sounded ideal, she was knowledgeable and very keen to ensure that if we agreed for her to take Bertina, she would have a good life. Luckily, as it transpired, she would be visiting Liverpool in the next couple of weeks, and we arranged to meet up to discuss things in more detail. She explained that she would need a little time to construct a large aviary and tick off a few more boxes but if we approved all should be ready in two or three weeks. Both Ann and I agreed that we would not find better and were relieved that at last we had finally found a new home for our sex change buzzard.

But that still left us with the dilemma of rehoming Bran the raven. Eventually someone aware of our dilemma gave us the contact details of a lady, again in Yorkshire, who ran a corvid rescue facility *(ravens, crows, rooks, jackdaws, magpies, and jays are all members of the corvid family)* and we wasted no time in making contact. She said that she would be delighted to offer Bran a new home and that he would be company for her own resident female raven. We informed her that Bran was quite a good mimic with his party piece being a rather posh 'Helloooooo' and 'Goodgoy' He never could pronounce his B's She explained that her own raven hadn't quite mastered the art of mimicry but hopefully would copy Bran once they were together.

In no time at all everything was in place for the pair of them to go to their respective new abodes. Bertina's new aviary was ready and waiting with the final formality being a signed declaration from Andy McWilliam (*at the time, Merseyside Police Wildlife Officer, later to become an Investigative Officer for the National Wildlife Crime Unit*) and myself that she was stolen from the wild as a chick and confiscated by court order. She was also a protected species under the Wildlife & Countryside Act 1981 and, due to being hand reared, deemed unsuitable for successful rehabilitation. It also stated that as a wild bred bird she could never be sold or used for commercial purposes.

With all formalities complete we were soon heading off to Yorkshire with Bertina safely confined to a travel box. The journey was uneventful, apart from at around the halfway point when she became restless in the confines of her box and at the first opportunity, I pulled into a lay by to check on her. Pulling on my falconer's glove I grasped the length of her green braided nylon leash protruding from her box. As I opened the door she immediately jumped onto my gloved fist and, with a few sorrowful squeaks, huddled tightly into me for comfort. As I gently comforted her an overwhelming feeling of connection flooded over me as though the bond of trust, and dare I say even affection (*definitely affection on my part at least*) that we had formed suddenly dawned on me and I came so very close to taking her back home. But she was going to a better life, and it would have been totally selfish of me to have taken that opportunity away from her. Once settled again I popped her back into her box and we resumed our journey north.

Some weeks later I received a letter from her new custodian to say how well she had settled in accompanied with a photograph of her perched in the treetops during a free flying exercise. Thankfully, it was the confirmation I needed to put my mind at rest in that I had made the right decision.

A couple of weeks later we were once again heading north with Bran where, on arrival, he was popped into his large new aviary. Before leaving we were introduced to a rather sleek attractive female raven who was destined to be Bran's partner, plus various other residents in the form of crows, magpies and jackdaws. A short while later we returned to Yorkshire to see how he was getting on and were relieved to find him content and happy particularly so in the fact that his solitary life was over, and he finally had the company of his own kind. We were informed some weeks later that his partner was now mimicking his vocabulary albeit in a Yorkshire accent.

But our responsibilities were not entirely over as we still had the three ancient owls, and even though they were still active for their age (*one of the tawny owls with a BTO leg ring was almost twenty years old!*) it didn't feel right to expect someone else to take responsibility for them in the knowledge that they could succumb to age related problems at any time. This of course left us with the dilemma of what to do with them. We had two options: one was euthanasia with the other to keep them in the hope that we just might find a place that at least had enough space to allow us to knock up a couple of smaller temporary aviaries until they finally fell off their perches.

Due to the fact that they still had a decent quality of life we decided on the latter.

At last, it felt that our final physical links to 2 Rangers Cottage had been severed and we could now depart with nothing other than a bucketful of memories plus a few chickens and three geriatric owls!

House hunting now became our number one priority, and we began to seriously search the properties for sale lists in North Wales. We were a bit on the fussy side and had put together a list of essential requirements. Number one being that it had to be a detached property with character in a rural setting. Number two, have a reasonably sized garden and garage space for our 1934 Hillman Minx, 1934 Austin 7 Nippy Sports and 1929 Austin 7 Chummy plus secure off-road parking for our modern mode of transport. Not an easy task! We quickly discovered that estate agents are extremely adept at making even the most run down of properties sound like a not to be missed opportunity, with pictures and a sales patter to create the impression that the place is twice as spacious and appealing as it really is.

One property we viewed was stated as being a detached period three bedroomed cottage of character consisting of a garage, a large garden and orchard, plus a stretch of river with exclusive fishing rights. In reality any period charm had long since been vandalised and the place was in dire need of a major face lift. A decrepit timber garage by the roadside was in an advanced state of being consumed by the creeping tentacles of ivy and a coating of green damp moss. The 'orchard' *(In inverted commas*!) consisted of half a dozen recently planted tiny apple trees with the river and its exclusive fishing rights down a near vertical fifty odd foot bank at the rear of the property where it would have been advantageous to have been adept at abseiling before attempting a fishing excursion! Needless to say, we didn't make an offer!

After another couple of unproductive viewings of equally embellished descriptions we were on our way to yet another viewing. We had just driven through a tiny village and were dropping down a slight hill to approach a sharp right-hand bend and as we did so had to slow down for a pony and trap trotting sedately on ahead. Eventually the driver signalled with his whip that he was taking a left down a side road signposted Little Rock, three miles. We immediately recognised the name as we had seen a property advertised there on Right Move but hadn't got around to arranging a viewing and as such decided on a detour to check it out. The narrow road meandered on with occasional passing places tucked tightly into the hedgerow. Sheep and cattle grazed in the fields beneath the Welsh hills carpeted with bracken, heather and gorse, their colours of green, purple, and yellow contrasting sharply with the thickets of woodland that dotted the hillsides, their trees of oak, rowan and pine leaning and stunted by a millennium of buffeting winds. Eventually the road began to climb a long gently rising hill bordered by woodland of tall slender ash and wild cherry until finally dropping down into the village of Little Rock.

The house was immediately on our left, raised quite high above the road and accessed by a rough track climbing through woodland finally reaching a five barred gate accessing the front of the property. Rather than drive up the track we dropped down to park on a patch of hard standing by a green potting shed and a wrought iron garden gate leading directly to a flight of steps and a steep meandering path leading through a well-manicured terraced garden to the house. To the left of the gate, another path climbed through an adjoining patch of woodland to the front of the house whilst to the right, a path led to the bottom section of garden with a large lawn, a mixture of various flowering shrubs and large ornamental conifers.

The house looked quite impressive with its west facing gable end and balcony overlooking the steep garden and beyond over the Vale. It also boasted a south facing conservatory whilst to the east, steep rocky woodland rose up towards limestone cliffs with heather and bracken clad hills beyond. It was without doubt the best we had seen so far with first impressions appearing to tick all the boxes. The location was good and not too far off the beaten track being only three miles from an historical market town consisting of a conglomeration of listed buildings lining its steep winding streets. The views were fantastic, the garden was large albeit rather steep, but to have our own patch of woodland was a bonus and something we hadn't even considered!

We wasted no time in arranging a viewing and the following week were being escorted around the house by the elderly owners. It was a three bedroomed detached, circa early 1800's, with two bathrooms, two staircases, a decent sized kitchen and dining room with panoramic views, plus a spacious living room with a large inglenook fireplace and double doors leading to the conservatory. Outside boasted a double garage with an attached utility room and of course the large garden with its adjacent woodland. Like most properties it had its pros and cons, but we liked it and wasted no time in arranging a second viewing after which we put in an offer, which was immediately declined. The following day after an evening of deliberation we submitted a second offer which this time was accepted, and the deed was done; we had at last bought ourselves a house in the wilds of North Wales!

At least this time, unlike our move from 1 Holme Head Cottage, Dunsop Bridge in the heart of the Forest of Bowland, to 2 Rangers Cottage, Thurstaston, on the Wirral, apart from a few chickens and three ancient owls we didn't have the menagerie of goats, dogs and a pony tagging along. But to say that we had no more ties to 2 Rangers Cottage wasn't strictly true in the respect that we still had an ex-resident from some years back in the form of a male tawny owl that returned every so often. He was originally brought in as a chick and hand reared to be eventually soft released over a period of many weeks from a very large natural aviary.

In due course he became totally independent, only returning for a free hand out in the depths of winter; that is until around early April of his second year in the wild he became much more regular with it becoming pretty obvious that he had found himself a mate and now had a family to provide for. He would usually arrive at dusk and perch in a large poplar tree in the garden where he would gaze through the living room window until we made a move towards the door whereupon he would fly onto the roof of his old aviary knowing full well that we would provide him with something to supplement his hunting. This went on for many years sometimes we wouldn't see him for weeks at a time whilst at others he was a nightly visitor. Occasionally his mate would accompany him along with their recently fledged chicks perched on the house roof, the chicks with their heads bobbing up and down as they gave off their high-pitched feed calls of *ke-suip, ke-suip, ke-suip*.

He was a textbook example of successful rehabilitation and brought us immense satisfaction and pleasure every time we saw him. But we were leaving, and I clearly remember one evening as I walked through the wooden gate by the now empty hospital unit as he perched no more than a metre above staring down at me with those big round dark eyes. I returned his gaze and with a heavy heart I remember saying that we would be leaving soon, and we would miss him terribly. At least we could take solace in the fact that he didn't really need us. He was now a truly wild owl that was more than capable of looking after not only himself but also his mate and their offspring. But that didn't alter the fact that we would miss him and the wonderful relationship of mutual trust. But we weren't going just yet as the legalities of purchasing a property had to be sorted out, plus a myriad of other tasks.

Thankfully, things went smoothly and a few weeks later we finally got the keys to our new home enabling us to set the wheels in motion for the move. One of the first tasks was to construct a large chicken pen on the bottom section of our new garden to accommodate our motley flock of fowl from rescued battery hens to a couple of miniature bantams, of which the cockerel, despite his diminutive size, could be as much a terror as the big cob swan! Eventually the day finally came when after some 28 years a removal van was once again parked outside 2 Rangers Cottage but this time not to unload but to transport our belongings to our new abode in North Wales; but we wouldn't be handing in the keys just yet!

In fact, despite the move, it would be some time before we finally gave notice to relinquish the tenancy of 2 Rangers Cottage. Eventually after weeks of commuting between the two houses transporting carloads of accumulated bits and pieces from my collection of musical instruments to potted plants and other paraphernalia plus driving across our three vintage cars we finally handed in the keys. I vividly remember the very last trip, I had loaded up the car with the last of the bulging packing boxes after locking the front door for the very last time and dropping the keys through the letterbox, I paused for a while to reflect on the past and as I did so an overwhelming sensation of total and utter silence enveloped me; not the normal quietness of peace and tranquillity that one often gets whilst sitting in the solitude of a garden or a spot miles from anywhere where birdsong is the only sound to break the silence. On the contrary, this was a strange, eerily intense silence that I couldn't comprehend. It was as though time itself had stopped and I was in a state of limbo. I remember looking around trying to catch a sound but nothing, you could have heard a pin drop! After what seemed an age but in reality, was probably only a minute or two the spell was broken and once again, I heard bird song and cars driving down the nearby road to the country park. Even now all these years later, the memory is as vivid as if it was yesterday. Perhaps someone out there may have a logical explanation for the experience, but I certainly don't!

What I did know was that it was the end of an era and my life as a ranger was over. I had come to the end of the final chapter. But as the last page closed a life with fresh chapters began that would lead me down a path that I couldn't have envisaged.

After all I was now officially retired with my days of working with wildlife and confronting badger diggers now a thing of the past. Or at least that's what I thought! But someone up there had other ideas and decided that I had a while to go just yet before finally hanging up my boots!

With 2 Rangers Cottage now completely cleared of our belongings and the keys handed in we had at long last cut the ties allowing us the freedom to settle into our new home without the constant hassle of travelling back and forth. The chickens had settled into their new pen constructed on a section of the large lawn at the bottom of the garden albeit not without a little hesitation at the beginning as, when first introduced rather than calmly exploring their new surroundings, they decided instead to fly over the wire and perch in the adjacent ornamental conifer trees. Eventually after a fair amount of cursing and chasing not to mention shrieks of objections from the chickens all were finally safely gathered up and locked away for the night in their coop. Thankfully when we let them out the following morning they were much more settled and soon busied themselves scratching around searching for a tasty morsel or two rather than heading off into the trees again.

The three geriatric owls were happy and content in their recently constructed large aviary in the wood and last but not least our 1934 Austin 7 Nippy Sports car was safely stored away in her newly built timber garage. Despite having a large double garage attached to the house we still had the predicament of having four cars and garage space for only two hence building a second one for the Nippy with the modern mode of transport designated to living outdoors.

As the weeks went by, we spent our time tending the large garden which we were now managing more for wildlife rather than aesthetic appearances with one of our first tasks being to set up a couple of bird feeding stations as well as incorporating a pond in what had been a lawn area both of which could be viewed from the conservatory. The previous owners used to scatter peanuts around in order to attract badgers which duly arrived for their regular nightly treats and, it goes without saying, that we were only too keen to continue the tradition.

Of course it wasn't all a one-way thing, the badgers got their treats, but it also allowed for some very comfortable badger watching! It was certainly an improvement to sitting out in a soggy field or perched precariously on a tree bough in a patch of woodland after dark trying hard not to shuffle about and ignore the discomfort of prolonged immobility or to stifle an irresistible urge to cough or scratch your nose which, of course, any one of which would send any self-respecting badger that may have finally made an appearance scuttling back underground never to be seen again.

Unfortunately, I tend to succumb to all of the above making my badger watching escapades a bit of a hit and miss affair! So, to watch badgers happily munching away on peanuts literally a few feet away illuminated by a security light whilst enjoying a coffee, or whatever else takes your fancy, in the warmth and comfort of a conservatory is very satisfactory indeed. But I must admit that as civilised as it may be there is nothing quite like badger watching for real, particularly as the light begins to fade and the smells and sounds of the night begin to sharpen your senses. The aroma of wood smoke drifting across from some distant cottage, the damp earthy smell of compost and decay of a woodland floor; a tawny owl calling whilst the repetitive bark of a fox becomes more distant as it travels through the night.

You wait with eager anticipation, eyes straining in the fading light as you wait for the distinctive black and white face to emerge from the sett. A full moon sends beams of yellow light to penetrate the woodland canopy casting dancing shadows to play tricks on your eyes. A cloud drifts across the moon shrouding everything in blackness, whilst the snap of a twig or the rustle of a leaf sets the mind racing as to what it might be, perhaps a fox stepping upon a twig or a wood mouse scampering amongst the leaf litter. Despite your eyes adapting a little to the darkness and the cloud finally drifting away allowing beams of moonlight to once more filter through the trees, your eyes and mind continue to play tricks on you. A moss-covered tree stump suddenly becomes alive, a tree takes on a form other than its own whilst every sound seems amplified. Despite the coldness of the night creeping into your bones and the aching of limbs from immobility coupled with the constant urge to scratch an itch, there is a magic around you and an overwhelming feeling of being drawn into this mysterious world and being at one with nature.

And then it happens! Suddenly a badger slowly emerges, its white facial stripe shining like a beacon out of the darkness as it takes in the night air, and you pray that your scent doesn't drift on the breeze to send it scurrying back underground putting an end to your endeavours. But no, it relaxes and ventures out to plonk its ample backside on the ground and leans back to relish in a good old belly scratch. One by one others begin to emerge, and as the brightness of the moon illuminates the scene you watch with wonder as the clan goes through their nightly ritual of scent marking and mutual grooming. Eventually some will amble off to go foraging in the pastures and hedgerows beyond in search of earthworms and cockchafer grubs or fruit such as wild strawberries and blackberries or if lucky they may stumble upon a wasp nest, which they will frantically dig out to get to the juicy grubs, seemingly oblivious to the stings from the angry insects.

Others busy themselves gathering fresh bedding, which they tuck under their chin and forelegs before dragging it backwards down into the sett. But if your badger watch is from late April through to summer you may be lucky enough to watch the antics of the cubs as they race and charge around like a gang of demented imps in the evening light often leading to their frolics becoming infectious with the adults joining in the fun. To watch a gang of cubs and adult badgers madly charging around in a game of 'catch me if you can' is delightful and more than makes up for the infuriating clouds of biting midges, the inevitable cramp, the ever frustrating urge to scratch an itch or the almost impossible task of stemming a cough, particularly after swallowing one of those blasted midges!

6

A Badger In A Snare, A Neighbour Checks Us Out & Otter Tracks In The Sand

Slowly but surely, as the weeks and months went by, we began to settle into our new home and put our own stamp on the place, particularly from a garden point of view. I was also capturing video footage of wildlife on my newly acquired trail cameras and diligently recording everything in my wildlife diary. Everything from the myriad of bird species to butterflies, bees, hoverflies, mice, voles and of course badgers and foxes all taking advantage of our blossoming wildlife garden was recorded.

Yes, wildlife was still very much an integral part of our lives but not from a nursing and rehabilitation point of view as in the past, but simply as a couple of keen naturalists. Our involvement with wildlife rehabilitation was in a past life and destined to be filed away in the history drawer, along with nearly thirty years of accumulated press cuttings, photographs, letters and old VHS videos of the many TV programmes filmed over the years. It was now merely something to reflect back on every once in a while, whilst enjoying a dram or two in front of the glowing embers of a log fire on a cold winter's night.

True, we missed the hands-on aspect of caring for a multitude of wildlife species on a daily basis, particularly badgers, but we had badgers here. We may not have been bottle feeding orphans or caring for sick or injured ones, but we had them trundling through the garden on a nightly basis plus we had many fond memories of hand rearing Toby, Pickles, Cassie, Milly and Kippy and their ultimate gradual return to the wild as a family group.

We often pondered over those times and of the many nights spent in the woods with them as they became familiar with their surroundings. Memories of Toby as he matured into adulthood and his eventual encounters with other badger clans. The overwhelming sadness at the sudden death of Kippy after almost two years of living as a wild badger. We had an absolute plethora of memories brimming with laughs, excitement, trepidation, happiness, and sadness. Ironically, our new home was a mere four miles away from their release site and it's not beyond the realms of possibility that the badgers visiting the garden could actually be descended from them. Now wouldn't that be extraordinary! But that was all in the past and as far as we were concerned, our hands on involvement with wildlife, particularly badgers, was a thing of the past.

But little did we know what was around the corner!

We were pottering around in the garden one afternoon when a local tree surgeon called round to say that whilst driving down a local lane, he had spotted a badger caught in a snare and could we help? Thankfully for whatever reason, I had kept hold of my animal graspers, thick animal handling gloves, a fairly large animal transporting carrier and a collapsible wire cage and wasted no time in loading all the necessary items into the back of his Land Rover Pick-Up truck to head off to the location. My main concern was that the badger, who obviously having been in the snare for some time could be seriously injured due to its attempts to free itself.

Some fifteen minutes later we pulled up by a steep embankment at the top of which was a barbed wire fence. The snare was on the field side and had been set on a well-worn badger path passing under the fence and down the banking. The badger was well and truly restrained with the snare wrapped tightly around its middle. Unfortunately, and to complicate matters, in its thrashing around to free itself it had become entangled in a mass of discarded barbed wire. The poor creature was exhausted and frightened. It was bad enough for it to have been out in broad daylight for many hours but to be painfully restrained firstly by the snare and then to be entangled in a mass of rusty barbed wire is incomprehensible!

We quickly transported everything from the Land Rover over the fence and into the field in preparation for the attempted rescue. The plan of action was that Ann would place the animal carrier with the door open and as close to the badger as possible while I restrained it with the animal grasper and with the wire cutters in my free hand attempt to remove the tangle of barbed wire leaving the final cut for the snare itself. Despite everything going on around him the badger stayed calm whilst I slowly but surely, strand by strand, removed the dreaded barbed wire to eventually reveal the snare attached firmly to a stake in the ground.

Unfortunately, it quickly became apparent that the hoop of the snare was tightly embedded around its tummy and buried beneath a thick coat of guard hairs. I came to the decision that I couldn't safely attempt to remove it under difficult field conditions and decided to firmly restrain it with the grasper whilst I cut the final length of snare wire attached to the stake whereupon once free I would, with one swift movement get the badger into the animal carrier.

Now that all sounds quite simple! But badgers are very adept at wriggling out of graspers and the last thing we wanted was for it to wriggle free and go trundling off down the field with the snare still tightly attached around its body. Thankfully, all went to plan, and we gave a huge sigh of relief as we closed the carrier door. With it safely secured we lifted everything back over the fence and down the bank to the back of the Land Rover and the journey home. Once home we placed the carrier and its occupant in the utility room where we managed to transfer it into the larger and more open collapsible wire cage whereupon we gave it a dish of water and covered the cage with a blanket.

We were now left with the predicament of ok, so far so good; but it still had the snare tightly secured around its middle which needed to be removed as soon as possible but the only way of doing was to sedate the badger. Once under sedation we could safely remove the snare and carry out a full examination to determine the extent of any injuries. Thankfully, Avril, a vet and colleague of Ann's lived in a village a few miles up the road and being at home on that particular day offered to pop down to sedate it followed by removing the snare, carry out an examination plus administering any treatment that may be required. Unfortunately, this was to prove to be a task much easier said than done!!

After administering the sedative through the cage into the badger's backside we retired to the kitchen for a coffee fully expecting to return thirty minutes later to the sound of snoring. But old Brock had other ideas and as we removed the blanket from over the cage it emitted a few intimidating growls and grunts showing not the slightest hint of being even remotely sedated. Avril decided to give it a second jab after which we once again retired for more coffee.

After a lapse of another thirty minutes, we returned once again to quietly remove the blanket this time fully expecting to see a fully comatose badger. But no such luck! It was obviously fighting the sedative and still very much fully alert. A third jab was out of the question and as such it was decided that I would place the grasper through the wire at the far end of the cage in an attempt to restrain it whilst Avril would enter the cage to crawl on hands and knees towards its backside armed with wire cutters in an attempt to remove the embedded snare.

Now as mentioned before, badgers and graspers aren't a great combination due to them being very adept at wriggling out of them. Anyway, in she went. The badger pulled back against the grasper, but not too hard and seemed fairly settled. Finally, with fingers probing for the snare, Avril managed to get the wire cutters underneath it but found it difficult to cut the wire. By this time, the badger decided that enough was enough and began emitting a low rumbling growl and twist and turn in an attempt to free itself from the grasper. I tightened the steel, plastic coated restraining cable as much as I dare but to avail! Suddenly with a sudden and violent twist of its head, it was free and spun around to face Avril who, with the speed of light backed out of the cage like a steam train in full reverse slamming the door tightly shut behind her.

At least the exercise determined that it didn't appear to have suffered any serious injury, but we were still left with the problem of removing the snare!

After a brief discussion plan number two was put into action where it was decided that Ann would take over grasper duties, whilst I crawled into the cage armed with the wire cutters. Luckily, I was able to locate and remove the snare quickly without too much fuss from old Brock and by some miracle it hadn't cut deeply into the flesh and with only superficial cuts. om the barbed wire

Avril administered a jab of broad-spectrum antibiotic (through the wire!) after which, we draped the blanket back over the cage and left it in peace.

That evening, just before dusk, we took it back to the location, lifted the cage and badger over the fence and placed them down by the badger path leading from the fence down through the field to a woodland copse. We left it for a few moments to settle before opening the door after which it cautiously came forward, paused on the threshold for a minute or two to take in the familiar smells drifting around on the evening breeze. As we watched from a distance, it slowly emerged, raised its head one more time to sniff the evening air. Suddenly as if the reality of its location and freedom finally dawned upon it, it rapidly vacated the carrier to trundle off across the field towards the patch of woodland and home.

That was one very lucky badger whose story could have been so different. The farmer was approached but without concrete evidence that he was the culprit, no further action could be taken but he was made well aware that any future incidents could be very different.

Little did we know it at the time but that was to be the start of many more years of involvement with badgers, not of rescuing and rehabilitating them as in years gone by and not only watching them through the conservatory window contentedly munching away on peanuts but of capturing hundreds of hours of trail camera video footage of their secret, nocturnal lives. I would write about them, give presentations about them and even be back on tele filming programmes about them.

The catalyst for all of that all started one day as I was pottering about in the bottom furthermost section of the garden when Ann called me (*I say called, at that distance it was more like an almighty bellow*) to say that we had a visitor. It was in fact a neighbour from down the road, a retired farmer who, along with his wife, lived at Garth Farm a rather impressive Grade II listed 17th century mansion house with an even older attached walled garden, plus an array of other ancient dwellings scattered around a rough cobbled yard, whilst an old watermill sat silent at the end of a hedge lined track.

The watermill last worked in the mid-1940s, with its great iron water wheel long since ground to a creaking halt and now slowly rusting away. The shattered windows were now boarded up with the ground floor littered with various paraphernalia from discarded wire and timber to an old weighing machine once used to weigh the bags of corn. But upon climbing the wooden stairs to the upper floor the beam of your torch penetrates the darkness to reveal a time warp of intact wooden workings of the old mill, now still and caked in years of grime and swathed in cobwebs.

Despite its dilapidated state, or should I say because of it, the mill provides a home, both temporary and permanent, to an array of wildlife from small tortoiseshell, red admiral and peacock butterflies hibernating away the winter months, to numerous species of spider and other insects. Spring sees the return of the lesser horseshoe bats to give birth to their single pup around July and August, whilst rabbits, fox, badger, wood mouse and other small mammals frequent the ground floor as the tawny owl snoozes away the day in the old adjoining cart shed. The estate also encompassed many acres of land from green pasture to bracken covered hill tops and areas of woodland, some of which border our own property.

After climbing the steep meandering path, I breathlessly reached the house to be met by a tall well-spoken elderly chap sporting a pair of binoculars and grasping a tall hazel thumb stick decorated with an assortment of badges.

Before I could utter a word, he strode towards me exclaiming in a strong authoritative voice, "Good morning, I'm John Harrop your neighbour from down the road, have you seen any bullfinches?"

I must confess that due to his stature, coupled with sharpness of tone and commanding voice, my initial inclination was to smartly jump to attention and salute, followed by barking, "No sir, can't say that I have!" But decided instead to respond with, "Hello, nice to meet you and sorry but no I haven't."

He then proceeded to enquire as to where we had come from, plus any other aspects of our previous life that he could prod out of us before residing in sunny North Wales.

Eventually after a thorough interrogation, he abruptly terminated the conversation with a "Jolly good, well done," followed by a quick about turn to stride off across the drive to climb into his old and somewhat battered Land Rover Defender, and with a slam of the door, followed by a plume of blue exhaust smoke, proceeded to trundle off down the track.

That was my very first introduction to Mr J. M. Harrop MBE and little did I know it at the time, but he and his wife Sue were to become much valued friends and neighbours. Over the coming years, John and I would spend many an evening in the old Landy trundling around the meandering narrow lanes of the Denbighshire countryside in search of various species of bat.

It soon became apparent that despite our totally opposite backgrounds we had common interests. He had been privately educated, an officer in the Welsh Guards and a gentleman farmer whereas yours truly was brought up on a council estate and educated (sort of!) at Ribblesdale Secondary Modern School. I served Queen and country as a squaddie in the Territorial Army, plus doing a variety of menial jobs, whilst endeavouring to achieve my goal of becoming a ranger. Another opposite end of the spectrum was that he was tall, and I somewhat vertically challenged!

But our mutual passion for all things wildlife plus a common interest in many other subjects swept away any hint of disparity regarding background with us spending many an hour sat around the farm kitchen table discussing a multitude of wildlife subjects, from badgers, otters to weasels and stoats to name but a few or a variety of other topics that held our mutual interest. And of course, our shared appreciation in all things appertaining to spirits. (*Purely in the liquid form and nothing to do with spooks and things that go bump in the night despite the fact that the old place was said to be haunted.*) We would often sample a dram or two of his finest single malt whilst putting the world to rights or watching badgers as they scrabbled onto the low stone ledge of his study window to retrieve a trail of peanuts.

As the months went by, we were discovering that this retirement lark wasn't at all bad. The garden kept us busy plus sorting out a few jobs on the house, and then of course there was the wildlife with badgers coming and going all night long as well as the bird feeding stations attracting a wide variety of species that had us constantly reaching for the binoculars. We were also very fortunate in that we could literally step out of the front door to climb the path through the woods and onto the hills above for a ten mile or so circular walk plus the fact that John and Sue allowed us unrestricted access to their land. Here we could wander at will through fields and by the banks of the meandering little river and of course the woods with their thoroughfare of well-trodden badger paths criss-crossing here, there, and everywhere, passing under long since fallen moss covered trees of Scots pine and ash.

John was born and bred at the farm and over the years had amassed quite an impressive list of various species of wildlife recorded on the land with everything from badger, fox, hedgehog, red squirrel, brown hair, and water vole to name but a few. He recorded that red squirrels were a breeding species up to 1953 when only one drey (*nest)* was found. He also recorded sighting the first grey squirrel in 1954 and confirmed breeding in 1959. A single red was seen again in 1955 with a final one in May 1962. Hedgehogs were a common breeding species in the 1960s, with frequent sightings of brown hare and good numbers of water vole in the slow-moving water ditches and the mill race (*canal*). Unfortunately, the population was wiped out in the harsh winter of 1962-63. Sadly, the red squirrel, brown hare and water vole have long since disappeared from the land with even the humble hedgehog now a rare sight.

His list of bird species was equally impressive with 34 breeding species recorded in 1957, including curlew, lapwing, skylark, barn owl and grey partridge. John carried out a similar survey in 2020, which sadly revealed a significant decline, with only 20 confirmed breeding species. But it's not all doom and gloom. Little egrets, although not breeding on the farm, are now recorded on an annual basis, as are mandarin ducks who have taken up permanent residency with goosander, kingfisher, dipper, and common sandpiper passing through. In December 2020, footage of a single water rail was captured on a trail camera, scuttling around the undergrowth on the edge of a pond below the big house, with further footage captured in 2021. A pair were also recorded on a daily basis on an overgrown stretch of the river from January to late March in 2022, but none at all through spring and summer.

In October 1962, John recorded finding a single dead lesser horseshoe bat, stating that it was the only definitive evidence of the species on the farm. By July 2022, over 70 were recorded roosting in the old mill and other outbuildings. Over the years, technology has moved on at an amazing pace with bat detectors and trail cameras making recording and monitoring wildlife so much easier and precise, and for me at least trail cameras have been (*and still are!*) an invaluable tool in monitoring and recording otters.

In his entire life of living and working the estate, John had never found evidence of otter so you can imagine his excitement when one day in December 2014 whilst walking the lower field below the homestead between the old pond and river he spotted what he thought could be otter tracks in a sand bank. Needless to say, he rapidly made for home to telephone me of his find and to ask if I could I get over there ASAP to check them out and hopefully confirm his suspicions.

I wasted no time in getting down there, and soon found myself looking at the distinctive five-toed, large, webbed footprints of an otter clearly embedded in the soft sandy bank by a bend in the meandering little river. To say he was pleased would be an understatement! Over the following days, Ann and I scoured the river and soon discovered more otter signs in the form of tracks by the water's edge and spraint deposited upon rocks and boulders. Otter poo and anal secretion, known as spraint, is black when fresh, turning grey with age. The poo will usually contain small fish bones and scales.

Since our move to North Wales, I have been using trail cameras to capture footage of the nocturnal creatures that passed through the garden after dark and wasted no time in setting one up under the old arched bridge across the river by the track to the farm. Upon returning a few days later I immediately spotted the fresh black tarry looking anal gland secretion, along with otter poo deposited on a rock by the water's edge, plus a jumble of otter prints ranging from large to small indicating that an adult with cubs had passed by. Upon checking the camera, I saw that it had been triggered on multiple occasions.

I quickly replaced the SD card, reset the camera, and made for home eager to see what had been recorded. And I wasn't to be disappointed! As the camera's SD card loaded the footage onto the computer, I quickly flicked through videos of blackbirds, robin and wren foraging on the bank during the day, along with a couple of mallard ducks sedately drifting by, and a heron stealthily scanning the water for a tasty fish or two. Then came the nighttime footage, with a couple of rats scampering around or swimming across to the far bank followed by the occasional wood mouse or vole and then bingo!! At 2.16 am on the 12th Dec 2014, an otter bitch and her two cubs came into view!

Mum occasionally emitted squeaks of reassurance to her offspring who, by their size and obvious insecurity, I guessed to be around four months old and probably only having recently left the safety and warmth of the breeding holt (*den*) to follow mum on her nightly forays. Otter cubs leave the natal den at around three months and despite being primarily aquatic mammals, otter cubs don't readily take to the water and take some persuasion from the bitch to actually do so. I wasted no time in setting up more cameras along the river in order to monitor the comings and goings of the otter family and it was a joy to watch as time went on to see the cubs becoming more confident and totally at one with their watery environment. Eventually the weeks turned into months until the cubs, male & female, were fully adept at chasing and catching fish and other prey. Despite their confidence they never wandered too far from mum and would give off plaintive calls of insecurity if she were out of their sight eagerly listening for her reassuring whistle.

They were such a close tightly knit family that it was difficult to believe that one day they would go their separate ways. Otter (*Lutra lutra*) cubs stay with mum for between seven to twelve months, by which time they are independent and at some point, will be encouraged to make their own way in life. If possible, I was keen to record the event which, thanks to the modern innovation of trail cameras, I was fortunate enough to achieve.

I last recorded them as a cohesive family group in the early hours of the 19th June 2015, once again under the bridge heading upstream. On the evening of the 20th June, the bitch was seen again heading downstream but this time alone. My first question was had the cubs dispersed or had something untoward happened? Hopefully time would tell and thankfully I didn't have long to wait as a week later, once again, the bitch was captured on trail camera under the bridge as she rested on the bank devouring a fish whilst on the opposite bank hiding behind a small bush was the female cub giving off the most pathetic cries imaginable. It soon became obvious that she wanted to approach mum but daren't, and despite her cries the mother completely ignored her. Eventually the cub plucked up the courage to leave the sanctuary of the bush and approach but as she did so the bitch immediately turned on her where, amidst a hullabaloo of high pitched squeaks and cries, giving one the belief that the cub was at the very least going to be licking a few nasty wounds. They rolled and tumbled around on the bank eventually ending up in the bush as the cub tried to retreat.

After what seemed an age when in reality it was only a few short minutes the bitch ceased her attack and returned to the river to swim upstream, leaving the cub pitifully whimpering in the bush. After witnessing what appeared to be a full-blown attack from the bitch towards her offspring you could be forgiven for fully expecting the cub to be seriously injured. But on the contrary, as soon as the bitch had departed the cub re-emerged and appeared to be none the worse for its ordeal. Despite what appeared to be a ferocious attack, it was in fact nothing more than mum getting the message across that it was now on its own. If my assumption of their age (*4 months)* when first recorded in December 2014 was correct, coupled with the six months of ongoing monitoring, would make a total of around ten months from birth to dispersal.

Nature can sometimes appear harsh but for the past ten months the cubs were her world. She suckled them, nurtured them, taught them everything they would need to survive in the wild and would have given her life to protect them. But like all kids, the time comes when they have to become independent and live their own lives. She would now have the freedom once again to travel farther afield through river and overland where eventually she would once again for a brief period at least, (*about seven days*) swim, dive and frolic with the big dog otter before he continued his wandering whereupon she would eventually return to the holt to raise a new family and the cycle of life would begin all over again.

Almost eight years have passed since I first followed the lives of that otter family and like them, I also continue to repeat the process. Otters are generally secretive, elusive creatures (*particularly on the waterways of England and Wales*) and despite my many years of following their comings and goings and of watching an otter bitch romp and play with her cubs to her final rejection at the time of dispersal, of following the wanderings of the dog otter as he journeys many miles through river, stream, ponds, lakes, ditches and fields patrolling his home range, they still constantly leave me in wonder at what they are going to reveal next. Or not reveal as is often the case!

There are a number of times a camera captures footage of an otter heading upstream, only for it not to be seen again despite the fact that for it to continue on its watery travels it will have to pass at least another four or five cameras. The only conclusion being that it's left the river and headed overland. Even more frustrating is the number of times I have followed a distinct otter track from the water to meander across a large open field where, infuriatingly, it suddenly stops as though the beast has been beamed up by a UFO from another universe! The dog otter in particular is very adept at running rings around my endeavours to keep an account of his wanderings.

As mentioned previously, we have a large, terraced garden managed primarily for wildlife, with the lower section being completely out of view from the house. We knew that we had a clan of badgers visiting (*more of badgers later)* on a nightly basis from a sett (*the Dickens clan*) situated in a section of woodland across the way. Their visits were so frequent that they had worn a well-defined path across the lawn and up the steep banking to the house as they trundled up for their nightly treat of peanuts, before heading off into the woodland to forage for a more natural diet. Out of interest I decided to put a trail camera down there basically just to monitor their nightly coming and goings. Now this is where the dog otter really starts to put two fingers up at me as when a few days later I decided to check the camera and replace the SD card. Later that day I popped the card into the computer to download the recorded footage and was totally gobsmacked to see that on the 2nd Feb 2022 at 6.38 am what should be nonchalantly trotting through the garden but the dog otter!! It's one thing to run rings around me in his own domain but to do it in my own garden, now that really is taking the Mickey!

Another interesting bit of footage from yours truly was of him surfacing from the depths to grab a mandarin duck and proceed to eat it on camera in broad daylight. The response from the audience when I include the video in one of my PowerPoint presentations, particularly when they see a flapping wing, is quite amusing with shocked gasps of, "Oh my goodness, the poor thing is still alive!" But you could find no better way of illustrating that the otter's diet is not restricted to fish alone plus it depicts nature in its truest form.

With so many new and exciting wildlife experiences, any initial reservations we may have had regarding retirement were quickly dissolved as wildlife was beginning to dominate our lives once more, with badgers and otters playing a major role. I was busy monitoring wildlife on my trail cameras and even field testing various makes and models for a company in North Wales, plus sitting on the Conservation Committee of the North East branch of the North Wales Wildlife Trust. I was also involved in certain aspects of the management of the woodland bordering the eastern boundary of our property known as Old Mansion Wood. It was originally part of the Garth Farm estate, but John had gifted it to the NW Wildlife Trust who now managed it as a nature reserve and at Johns request renamed it Wild Rock. It's a name that reflects the character of the area with its steep limestone wooded slopes climbing to a high rugged cliff top and limestone grassland with stunning panoramic views over the Vale.

Yep, life was ticking along nicely, but little did I know it then, but certain aspects of my past life were about to resurface with a vengeance!

Muffles, my very tame rescue fox

Velvet, Muffles' partner in mischief

Still from otter bridge

Investigating an incident of badger digging

Joint Police and RSPCA raid at Cwm Bowydd Farm and Hunt Kennels

System of artificial pipes and chambers at Cym Bowydd Farm and Hunt Kennels

Dickens the old boar badger arriving for his peanut treat

Filming ITV Wales Coast and Country

Filming for Badgers: Their Secret World

One of the No-Tail clan on the drive by the bench

One of the No-Tail clan on the drive by some peanuts

Close up of a badger taken with my camera mounted on a mini tripod, a 70 x 100 mm lens and cable release

Merseyside Police certificate of recognition

North Wales Police crime commendation award

7

A Copper Comes A Knocking, Badger Diggers & Court Cases

I briefly touched upon some of my escapades with badger diggers in Chapter Four and naturally assumed that upon leaving the ranger service any future contact with these Neanderthals would be well and truly over. After all, I was now officially retired, not only from the ranger service but also from assisting the police and RSPCA in investigating incidents of badger digging/baiting and being called upon to act as prosecution expert witness. How wrong I was!!

One morning in 2014, the telephone rang and upon picking up I heard, "Hello is that Mal Ingham?"

I replied that yes it was and how could I help?

"PC Dave Allen here from the North Wales Police Rural Crime Team. We have a badger digging case on the go and have been making enquiries to track down someone who may be able to advise and act as expert witness. Jim Ashley, chairman of Shropshire Badger Group, suggested I contact you" followed by "I appreciate the fact that you have recently retired from your wildlife ranger post but any chance you can help out here?"

I first met Jim some years ago through my work with badgers. At the time he was a Superintendent in the West Mercia Police Force and he and his wife were active members of the Shropshire Badger Group. Over the years we met up now and again, particularly as PC Simon Vaughan (*mentioned in Chapter Four*) had transferred from Merseyside to take up a position as a sergeant in the West Mercia force, with himself and his wife Michele now stalwarts of the Shropshire Badger Group.

I didn't know whether to curse or thank Jim for the recommendation but either way I could not refuse the request for help if it meant that I may be able to assist in bringing the badger digging morons to justice. The case was eventually heard at Mold Magistrates Court in Flintshire and thankfully presided over by a district judge. I say thankfully due to the fact that if my past experiences of magistrates are anything to go by, justice is far more likely to be handed out by a district judge. Unfortunately, this was an opinion that would only be strengthened in the coming years following further experiences of magistrates not appearing to understand the severity and total criminality of the crime and finding badger diggers not guilty despite all the evidence proving otherwise.

I had considered all the facts presented to me by the police, culminating in my submitting an in-depth expert report and now here I was, some months later, sat alone in a witness room at Mold Magistrates Court awaiting to be called to give my evidence. Despite having given expert evidence on numerous occasions over the years in both magistrate and crown court the butterflies in my stomach were still having a field day.

The nervous trepidation endured whilst awaiting the inevitable call of, 'Mr Ingham to the stand please' never seems to diminish with time.

Time drifted slowly by as I sat there awaiting the call and the appearance of the usher to escort me into the court room and wondering what the delay may be. Every now and again I would wander over to the window to stretch my legs or to help myself to yet another cup of chilled water from the dispenser in the corner of the room. But I was conscious of the fact that if I drank too much, coupled with the nervous tension, I would run the risk of being in dire need of a pee just as I was called to the witness box.

To be cross examined by the defence is bad enough but to be desperate for a pee at the same time isn't conducive with keeping the mind sharply focused on the matters at hand. I had of course experienced all of these emotions before and not just in relation to giving evidence.

In my parachuting days I would often find myself killing time in the long wooden building that served as the parachute centre whilst downing yet another mug of coffee as I awaited the call of Ingham! Get your kit on,' whereupon I would pull on my parachute, buckle up the harness, followed by safety checks, before finally plonking my backside on the wooden bench by the runway awaiting the order to approach and board the aircraft. Now once you have zipped up your jump suit, coupled with the harness and straps that attach the parachute to your person, going for a pee at this point in time can be equated to Houdini attempting to free himself from shackles and chains!

And yes, you have guessed it! On more than one occasion I would get the order to board just as my brain and bladder told me I wanted a pee. But at that late stage a pee was out of the question even if you could have managed to free yourself from the conglomeration of restraints. Unfortunately, you were left with no alternative but to climb on board and sit cross legged until the required altitude was reached and you were over the drop zone. At this point the engine revs slowed and the adrenalin began to pump as you awaited the order from the jump master to make for the door and the thumbs up to launch yourself into space to eventually land on terra firma once more, gather up your parachute and if the urge was still there, dump your chute in the packing room and make a dash for the loo.   Thankfully more often than not, the urge was merely psychological, brought on by the nervous tension of leaping out of an aeroplane yet again. All of which was quickly replaced by a feeling of pure exhilaration as your chute deployed and you drifted sedately down until once again the pangs of apprehension and trepidation crept in as the ground rapidly came up to meet you. Needless to say, any lingering thoughts of wanting a pee tended to evaporate rather quickly as you concentrated on a pain free landing. Anyway, I digress, back to the witness waiting room.

I had probably been sat there twiddling my thumbs for a couple of hours and in an attempt to relieve the tedium I must have read every poster adorning the walls plus the assortment of leaflets neatly laid out on the small round table explaining the ins and outs of being a witness and court procedure when at last in strode the court usher his black gown flowing behind him. My brain immediately went up a gear as it prepared for the short walk to the court room and the inevitable grilling from the defence as they attempted to discredit my report. But he hadn't arrived to escort me anywhere but merely to apologise for the delay and to inform me that the defence and prosecution were in consultation and that he would keep me updated.

Another thirty minutes or so passed by before he returned. This time to inform me that I would not be called to the stand after all as the defendants had submitted a last-minute guilty plea and that he would now escort me to the court room as the district judge would like to address me. The judge thanked me for my evidence stating that it assisted him greatly in bringing the case to a successful conclusion.

In January 2015, I received a letter from North Wales Police Deputy Chief Constable thanking me for my assistance in the case.

It read as follow -

Dear Mr Ingham,

I have been informed by PC David Allen, Rural Crime Officer that you have played a significant part in helping to bring an organised gang from Liverpool who were committing wildlife crime in our local community to justice.

From reviewing the information received from PC Allen I understand that you acted as an expert witness throughout the investigation. Your support in this investigation also required you to attend court to provide expert advice. I am grateful for all the support you gave to this investigation and your attendance at court which was all done in your own time.

As a result of your support with this investigation both defendants received 160 hours community service, £300 costs and £65 surcharge. Their equipment, including a specialist off road Land Rover Discovery, was also forfeited.

I wish to take this opportunity on behalf of myself and North Wales Police to pass on our sincere thanks to you in respect of your actions. Your dedication and commitment in helping to bring this organised gang to justice is much appreciated.

Signed

Gareth Pritchard

Dirprwy Brif Gwanstabl / Deputy Chief Constable

The sentence may seem lenient, amounting to nothing more than a slap on the wrist particularly considering the abhorrent cruelty these people inflict on animals whilst satisfying their sadistic inclinations. But the forfeiture of their equipment including a Land Rover Discovery would have been a significant sting in the tail but if my past experiences regarding the mentality of badger diggers and baiters are anything to go by, it wouldn't deter them for long before they are back out there with their dogs and spades.

Badger baiting was made illegal in 1835 under the Cruelty to Animals Act along with bear baiting and cock fighting. (*Cock fighting wasn't banned in Scotland for another 60 years*) And here we are, almost two centuries later with badger baiting being as rife now as it was then. (*Even cock fighting continues but tends to be less blatant than badger baiting.*) Further limited protection was afforded to the badger under the Badger Act of 1973 which proved to be so ineffective that it served no real purpose with badger digging / baiting and the destruction of badger setts being as rife as ever regardless of the act. The Badger Protection Act came into force in 1991 and in 1992 the Badger Act of 1973 and 1991 were consolidated into the Badger Protection Act 1992.

The maximum custodial sentence for someone convicted of badger digging or baiting under the 1992 Protection of Badger Act is a paltry 6 months, a maximum fine of £40,000 or both. Plus of course a court can order confiscation of any equipment including vehicles and dogs plus issuing a ban on keeping dogs for a couple of years or more.

After reading the above you can be forgiven for thinking that ok, the courts may have their hands tied regarding dishing out a lengthy custodial, but they can certainly hand out a whacking fine, plus confiscations and a ban on keeping dogs!

But in reality, the perpetrators, if found guilty, very rarely receive anything like that with a few weeks custodial and a fine of a couple hundred quid plus court costs being the most likely outcome. Or even more insignificant, a Community Service Order!

Badger digging and baiting are cruel pastimes often resulting in the dogs suffering horrendous injuries which in practise means that the courts, depending on circumstances can hand out a maximum of 5 years custodial for cruelty to the dogs under the Animal Welfare (Sentencing) Act 2021. It really is a bizarre situation when anyone inflicting cruelty to a badger only faces a maximum of 6 months custodial whilst anyone inflicting cruelty to a domestic animal can face up to 5 years, which in itself is pathetic considering some of the horrendous cruelty inflicted on domestic animals.

So, what has the Badger Protection Act of 1992 actually achieved? To be perfectly honest, not a lot! Yes, in theory at least it affords the badger and his home legal protection but like the Badger Act of 1973 it serves as no real deterrent to anyone wishing to inflict harm on the badger or disturb his home. The sick minded individuals out there who get their kicks out of inflicting the most horrific cruelty will only begin to think twice if they know that if caught and convicted they run the risk of a lengthy term at His Majesty's pleasure plus a hefty fine, this also applies to those who blatantly block, damage or destroy a badger sett.

If and when the Badger Protection Act of 1992 is finally brought in line with the maximum penalties under the Animal Welfare Act and the courts finally begin to impose maximum penalties will we hopefully see a decline in the barbaric pastime of badger digging and baiting.

In years gone by during my many face-to-face confrontations with badger diggers and baiters, a report of an incident more often than not came from a member of the public. The usual scenario was that I was often the first on the scene and having to observe from a safe distance until back up arrived in the form of a police constable. It was quite normal in those days for the officer to be completely out of his comfort zone and totally oblivious of the existence of the Badger Protection Act 1992.

It certainly wasn't unusual for the officer to ask me if a crime had actually been committed despite the fact that these guys were equipped with spades and terrier dogs and caught red handed in the act of digging a currently active badger sett.

This wasn't a case of blatant ignorance or indifference from an officer, it was merely the fact that they were just not taught anything about wildlife crime and the various animal welfare acts. They were decent coppers but, in these situations, and through no fault of their own, they found themselves totally out of their depth. But many, once they realised the appalling cruelty these individuals inflicted on animals, plus their blatant disregard for anyone of authority, were more than keen to assist and to familiarise themselves on the Badger Act and other wildlife protection laws.

I have been spit at, verbally abused, and threatened to have my head caved in with a spade by diggers and on one occasion even had threats of violence made towards me by a digger whilst being interviewed under caution. Due to that particular incident, I was put under police protection for a few months resulting in me being given a rapid response telephone number in case of trouble and the occasional police car cruising around our property after dark. On more than one occasion upon leaving Wirral Country Park visitor centre, I would spot a police car parked close by. Badger diggers and baiters are your typical bully boys who, when confronted on a one to one basis, are nothing more than a bunch of whimpering cowards and as such I tend to take any threats verbal or physical as nothing more than pathetic bravado but on this occasion the police decided it was wise to play safe and keep a watchful eye on me.

The change of attitude by the police to wildlife crime was a gradual process but over time they began to place more emphasis on the subject with me being invited give a presentation to probationary officers in the Police HQ in Liverpool, particularly with regards to badger digging and baiting and the Badger Act. The presentation went down well, with them all genuinely sickened by the so-called sport. One very large probationary officer apologized for having to leave the room during one particular harrowing section of the presentation but soon returned biting at the bit to get his hands on them. Eventually Merseyside police incorporated the role of police wildlife crime officer into the normal day to day duties of an inspector. It was at best nothing more than a token gesture but at least it was better than nothing. He had only recently been given the duties when I was called to an incident of sett destruction which required his presence. To give credit where it's due, he immediately drove over from Liverpool to meet me at the location.

As I waited by my Land Rover, an unmarked car eventually pulled up alongside and a dapper gentleman in a blue pin striped suit got out and proceeded to don a pair of wellies and retrieve an umbrella from the cars boot, before striding over to introduce himself. He wasn't at all what I expected and looked more like a city banker than a police inspector. But despite appearances, I was impressed by his approach to the incident. Unfortunately, he retired a few months later and I was back to square one with regards to not having access to a police officer whose duties involved dealing with incidents of wildlife crime. Thankfully within a few months he was replaced by not one, but two officers. A sergeant and an inspector and this time stationed on the Wirral. But frustratingly, like their predecessor, their wildlife crime responsibilities were merely incorporated into their normal everyday duties.

Yes, they were genuinely keen and interested, but once again and through no fault of their own, they were not particularly familiar with the various laws relating to wildlife protection. Frustratingly due to their full-time duties combined with their shifts, they were almost impossible to get hold of when needed. Tragically the sergeant was badly injured in a car accident whilst responding to a call (*not associated with wildlife*) resulting in him sadly having to retire from the force. The inspector eventually became a part time ranger but his full-time role as a police inspector still greatly restricted his availability to respond to incidents of wildlife crime. But thankfully things were about to change for the better!

Merseyside Police decided to appoint another wildlife crime officer in the form of Detective Constable Steve Harris al. t, once again, as an extension to his normal everyday duties. But he wasn't working shifts, and he was keen and readily available.

And then things got even better in the form of a full-time wildlife crime officer in the form of Police Constable Andy McWilliam, based at Crosby police station. Andy was a keen ornithologist with a strong interest in all things relating to the investigation of wildlife crime. (*Andy is previously mentioned in Chapter Three.*).

As you can imagine, this combination of two wildlife crime officers was a vast improvement with regards to tackling wildlife crime in Merseyside. The three of us worked together virtually on a weekly basis investigating everything from badger persecution to raptor crime. Andy eventually retired from the force and subsequently became an Investigative Officer for the National Wildlife Crime Unit where we continued to work closely, particularly with me assisting in warrant raids appertaining to birds of prey. Eventually after serving his thirty years, Steve also retired who, like Andy, continued the fight against wildlife crime and animal cruelty by becoming the League Against Cruel Sports Head of Enforcement and Legal Resources.

And then of course I retired but not before the two of them surreptitiously got me into Merseyside Police HQ on the pretext of attending a seminar. I should have realised that something was afoot as Steve seemed overly keen that I attend even to the point of offering to taxi me over there. Anyway, off we went, and on arrival we signed in and proceeded to climb a flight of stairs passing an array of cabinets displaying various police paraphernalia from around the globe to eventually arrive at the designated lecture room. A low stage with a large projector screen dominated the front, whilst a white melamine tripod flip chart sat to its side. Blue fabric covered conference chairs were neatly lines in rows, each provided with an A4 folder containing info on the various aspects of the seminar.

The room was quite noisy with the rattling of chairs and general chit chat as people arrived and made for a vacant seat. As soon as we entered, Andy took hold of my arm and led me through the hustle and bustle to three reserved seats on the front row which I thought odd as no other seats appeared to have been reserved. On the contrary, it seemed more of a free for all on a first come first served basis. Anyway, we plonked ourselves down and eventually with everyone else seated the Deputy Chief Constable took the stage. A hush fell over the room apart from the occasional shuffle or a muffled cough.

After welcoming everyone to the seminar plus saying a few words on the general content, he finally said, "I have one last duty to perform before I formally open the proceedings," followed by, "will Mr Malcolm Ingham please step onto the stage."

To say I was gobsmacked would be an understatement! Anyway, up I went wondering what on earth was coming next whereupon he shook my hand and presented me with a Merseyside Police 'Certificate of Recognition Award' after which, we posed for the obligatory photographs and as I glanced down from the stage, I saw the smug smiling faces of Andy and Steve.

I had been well and truly set up!

And to emphasise the fact even more and almost to the day, some twenty years later I was awarded the North Wales Police & Crime Commissioners Rural & Wildlife Champion Award. But despite the passing of time.

That was over twenty years ago way back in 2002, and if anyone had told me then that I would still be confronting badger diggers and baiters, and giving expert evidence twenty years later I would not have believed them. But here I am, and still doing it! The diggers and baiters are just as busy and as cruel and sadistic as they ever were but thankfully the police's approach to rural and wildlife crime has changed dramatically over the past few years and particularly so here in Wales. Prior to 2013 most police forces would have had at least one officer assigned either full or part time to deal with wildlife crime. But one or even two full time dedicated officers, particularly in a large rural county, would be run off their feet attempting to deal with the seemingly never ending incidents of fish and deer poaching, badger digging, raptor persecution, hare coursing, habitat destruction, farm theft, cattle and sheep rustling, sheep worrying and fly tipping to name but a few.

In 2007, Rob Taylor of the North Wales Police was appointed as the sergeant attached to the Countryside Council for Wales, with the brief to investigate species and habitat offences. Prior to this Rob had served on the forces helicopter, been a traffic sergeant and a hostage negotiator along with other police roles. To assist him he had a few part time wildlife officers to call upon but in Rob's own words, it was a very ad hoc affair. In 2013 Rob was approached on behalf of the Police Commissioner to set up the first UK dedicated Rural Crime Team in North Wales. This was groundbreaking in the realms of tackling the issue of rural and wildlife crime and once up and running, would be the very first such team in the UK. Rob's first task was to appoint four full time police constables, with one being attached to Natural Resources Wales. Following a formal process of selection in 2013, the team was finally formed with Rob as team manager. It had the key role of tackling the very real issue of rural and wildlife crime. It soon became a great success with many investigations leading to prosecutions, so much so, that other forces followed the lead in setting up their own dedicated teams.

Rob retired from the police in 2016 and was subsequently awarded the Queens Police Medal in the Queens 90th birthday honours list. But that wasn't the end for Rob, as three short weeks later he returned once again as manager of the team but this time in a civilian capacity. In 2017 he was given the task of forming and managing a second dedicated team, this time in the

Dyfed Powys force which subsequently led to him training a third team in Gwent. I also became involved in the training of these officers along with the North Wales team with regards to evidence gathering and recording at the scene of a badger digging incident. In 2021, Rob was given the role as the very first Wales Rural & Wildlife Police Crime Co-ordinator, a role that was initially for a period of twelve months but extended for another three years in 2022. The only downside was that to accept the extension he had to resign from the North Wales force and join the South Wales Police, but he certainly left a lasting legacy!

Little did I realise it at the time but that badger digging case at Mold magistrate's court was to be the first of many over the coming years with me being asked to assist in investigations and called to give expert court evidence in both North and South Wales and even travelling as far as Carlisle in Cumbria.

A job would usually begin with a call on my mobile with number withheld and the voice of PC Dave Allen saying, "Dave here mate, we've got a job we would like you to look at," followed by a few brief details and location.

Upon responding to a report of a badger digging/baiting incident it's regarded as good practise by the police to have the area examined by an expert within twenty-four hours to carry out a survey to determine if the area in question is a currently active badger sett. Any evidence gathered after the twenty-hour period could potentially be classified as non-admissible. But regardless of that, the quicker I can be at the scene and begin my job of surveying the area the better. Inevitably the scene will most likely have suffered major disturbance, firstly from the actual digging and the trampling of feet by both human and dogs and secondly by anyone else who may have approached the scene prior to my arrival.

My first task is to take a What3Words code of the location followed by making a sketch map of the area whilst being careful not to add further disturbance. Once completed I will have decided where to begin my examination which would usually be a hole where signs of obvious digging had taken place. An evidence number marker would be placed by the hole followed by two thirty-centimetre rulers showing the height and width. A typical badger hole is generally in the shape of an inverted D measuring roughly thirty centimetres by 30 centimetres. After taking a photograph I will begin to look for badger hair in the spoil thrown out by the badgers, plus badger footprints or claw marks and anything else that can be classified as evidence of current badger activity at the time of my visit. I will photograph badger paths and badger hair where the path goes under a fence or brambles. I will look for latrines and anything that the diggers may have discarded such as a cigarette stub, beer bottle or can etc. which could hold vital DNA or fingerprints.

Each piece of evidence will have its own individual marker number followed by an in-situ photograph prior to being collected and bagged. This procedure is repeated all around the area until I'm confident that a thorough survey has been conducted and I haven't overlooked any potentially vital piece of evidence. The location of both dug and undisturbed holes plus badger paths, latrines, and anything else of relevance is jotted down in my notes with locations added to my sketch of the area.

The next stage is to write up my report and this is where the correctness of everything noted on site is vitally important. My objective is that anyone reading the report will be able to get a clear picture of the area and the events that had taken place on and around a currently active badger sett. The North Wales Rural Crime Team work in close partnership with the RSPCA Special Operations Unit and as such, despite the police's initial involvement, it can often be that the RSPCA will actually take the prosecution.

The duration of a badger digging/baiting court case can be anything from two to three days and is an expensive undertaking at the best of times and even more so if you lose! Before deciding to commit themselves to taking a case, the RSPCA have to be fairly confident that the prosecution evidence is pretty solid plus faith in the expert witness's ability to withstand defence cross examination. Hence the importance of ensuring that my evidence and report is as solid as it possibly can be. To submit a weak or inconclusive report would be deemed as too risky to take to court, with the consequences being that a gang of badger diggers/baiters, despite being caught red handed, walk away with smiles on their faces and waving two fingers in the air.

Once a report is submitted and been accepted as strong enough to proceed to court, then it's a waiting game. It can be many months after submitting a report before the official letter from Criminal Justice Service arrives informing me that my presence as a witness is required along with court dates and venue. At some point prior to that, I will have received a copy of the defence expert witness's report along with comments regarding its content. Obviously being on opposite sides, he or she will usually state that, 'Mr Ingham wouldn't know a badger if he fell over one, or a badger sett from a rabbit warren.'
Or words to that effect. The next stage being that I respond to the contradictions and general negativity.

It's all very much a game, and if the crime of badger digging and baiting wasn't so heinous, with the defendants being nothing more than cruel, sadistic morons it would be amusing, but in reality, it's anything but!

I have been coming up against the same defence lawyers for many years, and despite the fact that they are defending these people they are, in the main at least, professional and generally courteous. Yes, they will give you a bit of a grilling, that's their job, but they are not vindictive or overly aggressive in their cross examination. And then of course there are the complete opposites!!! But more of them later.

For now, let's go back to the defence expert witness.

I first came across this particular individual many years ago whilst giving expert evidence on a badger digging case in Staffordshire. The defence lawyer at the time, an old adversary of long standing who in the past employed an expert witness who went by the name of The Reverend & Worshipfulness, Prof, and Doctor Pea. (*Or something similar*) In 2014, he was covertly filmed by a BBC Panorama undercover reporter who was purporting to be a badger digger worried that he had been filmed whilst digging a sett and approached the Reverend & Worshipfulness, Prof, Doctor Pea for advice on a defence.

He was advised that for a substantial fee his Worshipfulness etc. etc. could give a favourable expert statement followed by exclaiming, "what you have done and what they can prove are two different things."

Obviously when this entered the public domain, he very quickly vanished off the scene, only to be replaced by another, who from here on in will be referred to as Leemax. He was a veterinary surgeon and farmer with a diploma in law. Unfortunately like his predecessor he was seriously lacking in the principles and integrity department and very adept at twisting evidence to suit the defendants. Sadly, like many who defend these people, he was part and parcel of the hunting fraternity who, from what I often witnessed in court, appeared to be totally at home in the company of diggers and baiters, or indeed anyone else who participated in illegal wildlife persecution.

It's only fair to add at this point that not all who participate in country sports are of the same mentality but sadly my many first hand experiences of the sadistic cruelty often inflicted on wildlife in the name of sport, particularly with regards to foxes and badgers, have inevitably influenced my opinions and made me just a tad pessimistic!

8

A Badger Baiting Hunt Master

After the successful conclusion of the Mold badger digging case and receiving the letter of appreciation from the North Wales Police Deputy Chief Constable, I fully expected that to be a one-off incident and the grand finale to my days of confronting badger diggers and baiters and giving prosecution evidence. But, like a lot of things since my retirement from the ranger service, my past life appeared to be refusing to fade into the realms of history as people and circumstances seemed to be continuously reawakening it.

Obviously, I relished my continued involvement with wildlife, particularly being out and about checking my ever-increasing number of trail cameras scattered around Garth Farm monitoring otters and badgers. I had also acquired a couple of Mostela small mammal boxes *(Mostela boxes were initially designed to capture trail camera footage of stoats and weasels. The animal enters via a pipe which is partially cut away to allow entry into the box itself whilst a trail camera is placed at the opposite end to record their comings and goings.)* I modified the boxes by cutting away a section of the hinged roof and incorporating a clear Perspex window which allows natural light into the box to record not only in infra-red but also daylight colour footage. The cameras, like the boxes, were slightly modified by blue tacking a + 2 close up lens over the camera's existing lens allowing for much clearer close-up images.

I placed the boxes at the foot of a dry-stone wall in the wood by the house and to date they have recorded weasel, wood mouse, house mouse, bank, and field vole, common, pigmy and water shrew, common frog, toad, wren, and blue tit plus a variety of spiders and woodlouse. On the 1st July 2023, a shrew was captured on camera that appeared different from the other three. After playing the video back a few times, I came to the conclusion that it could possibly be a Greater White-toothed shrew! The Greater, White-toothed shrew (*Crocidura russula*) can be found on Guernsey, Alderney and Hern but not thought to be on mainland Britain until recently discovered in Sunderland. The Mammal Society were asking for other possible records and as such I sent them the footage. They quickly got in touch to say that one of their experts had confirmed that it was indeed a Greater White-toothed shrew.

A couple of days later they contacted me again this time to say that to be 100% sure they wanted a second opinion. Unfortunately, the second expert was no committal and couldn't decide one way or the other. I haven't seen it since and the record, for the moment at least, is unconfirmed.

One small mammal that despite being recorded on a regular basis on camera outside the box, but as yet hasn't actually gone in, is the stoat.

I have another camera set up by a large water bath in the wood which attracts an absolute plethora of wildlife from badger, fox, stoat, and rabbit to the diminutive wood mouse. But it really comes up trumps with regards to bird species with everything from your common or garden birds to marsh tit, great spotted woodpecker, nuthatch, buzzard, sparrow hawk and on the 14th February 2023, a juvenile goshawk!

I often ponder over the fact on how beneficial trail cameras would have been in my wildlife rehabilitation days. They would have been an invaluable tool for monitoring wildlife making the transition from captivity to the wild but in those far off days they were just not around!

I think it fair to say that we were quite enjoying this retirement lark. The garden's transformation from an overly manicured one to one more in harmony with wildlife was coming along nicely. My trail cameras were keeping me busy and with the Mold badger digging case over and done with I was taking comfort in the fact that my involvement with investigating wildlife crime and giving expert prosecution evidence was history. I had never relished attending court and always approached it with a degree of trepidation and a sigh of relief when it was over and done with, at least until the next time. But now thankfully there would be no next time.

Or at least that was the plan!!

It was around 10am on Tuesday, 7th February 2017 and I was in the conservatory enjoying a mug of coffee whilst watching the hustle and bustle of a myriad of bird species all taking advantage of a free handout at my bird feeders when my ornithological respite was rudely interrupted by the ringing of the telephone. As I grudgingly swapped binoculars for telephone, recollections of the Mold case came flooding back to haunt me as I heard once again the dulcet tones of PC Dave Allen.

"Morning Mal, Dave here from the Rural Crimes Team. Sorry to bother you, mate, but any chance you can give us some assistance in a warrant raid in the morning?"

Apparently following a tip off, the RSPCA's Special Operations Unit had carried out a covert surveillance operation at the Dwyryd hunt kennels and farm in Blaenau Ffestiniog in Gwynedd, North Wales. Not only had they captured video footage of horrific domestic and farm animal cruelty but on the 5th February captured footage of badger baiting, all of which resulted in a warrant raid on the premises. He went on to explain that if I was available a police car would pick me up at 06.00 hours to take me to Blaenau Ffestiniog Police Station for a briefing.

I knew only too well that to agree to the request would involve a day of meticulous examination of the site of the badger baiting, as well as recording and photographing evidence, followed by the time-consuming process of putting it all together in a lengthy report. This would eventually culminate in my least favourite pastime of being summoned to court to give expert evidence and the inevitable cross examination by the defence. Despite the knowledge of what I was letting myself in for, I could not refuse and as such I was up bright and early the following morning. After loading my rucksack with all the necessary requirements including the vital lifesaving flask of coffee and sandwiches, I made my way down the rough track to the roadside to await my transport.

It was a fine, cold, dark morning with the moon not quite full but bright and clear enough to light my way as it filtered through the overhanging branches of wild cherry, ash and sycamore. As I reached the end of the track, a tawny owl silently glided from the trees to the wood across the road as the headlights of a patrol car came round the bend to illuminate the scene.

As it pulled up an officer climbed out with a "Morning Mal, just hang fire for a tick whilst I move this lot out of your way." He then proceeded to remove a cardboard box overflowing with various items of police paraphernalia from the passenger seat and pop them in the back. I climbed aboard and, with seat belt securely fastened, off we went.

Dawn was just about breaking as we pulled into the car park at Blaenau Ffestiniog Police Station. Parking was at a premium with RSPCA vans and police cars virtually taking up every available space. Eventually we squeezed into a vacant spot and entered the station to be escorted into a briefing room. The place was crammed to the gunnels with police and RSPCA Special Ops Unit personnel, some of whom had travelled overnight to be there.

Rob Taylor and Chief Inspector Ian Briggs from the RSPCA Special Ops Unit briefed everyone on the operation and the designated roles of individual teams with my task being to examine and gather evidence in a small woodland area where the badger baiting had been covertly filmed, whilst the rest concentrated on other animal cruelty/welfare issues. It was explained that two raids were taking place with the first at a premise in Llandudno where, once confirmation of it being successfully executed and with individuals in custody, the raid at the Dwyryd hunt kennels and farm would begin. As we waited for the word to go some mingled and chatted whilst others just sat in silent contemplation.

Ian Briggs had been a Chief Inspector with the Special Ops Unit for some time, and we had previously worked together on a number of occasions in years gone by but hadn't seen each other for quite a while.

After the briefing he wandered over and, as we shook hands, exclaimed, "Didn't expect to see you here Mal, heard on the grapevine that you had retired."

I responded with the clarification that yes, I had indeed retired but obviously the police had other ideas.

The conversation was suddenly cut short as confirmation came through that the first raid had been successfully executed with individuals apprehended and dogs and equipment seized. With that it was all go as people flowed out into the car park to jump into their respective vehicles and make their way in convoy to the farm. It was only a short journey and within ten minutes or so our convoy was heading down a rough winding track into the remote Bowydd Valley overshadowed by the craggy hills and long since defunct slate quarries still shrouded in the low damp mist of early morning. Eventually we entered a large farmyard dominated by a period two storey stone and slate farmhouse sat amidst a conglomeration of other buildings, some of which were old and dilapidated. Their stone walls stained green with mildew whilst moss and algae sprouted between the cracks where mortar had crumbled. Others were of a more recent construction consisting of corrugated sheeting around a framework of steel girders. Various bits of farm machinery and vehicles lay as if abandoned around the yard with the surrounding land consisting of rough, damp, undulating pasture whilst a stream meandered its way at the rear of the farm to continue its journey along the valley floor. Sheep and a couple of ponies grazed on what they could find amongst the rushes and coarse grass.

As we parked up and alighted from our respective vehicles, the RSPCA Inspectors split into groups to search the hotchpotch of buildings, whilst the police headed to the house to issue the warrant. The slamming of vehicle doors set off a frenzied barking and wailing of dogs adding to the already tense atmosphere.

As I stepped from the car to change into my wellington boots and retrieve my gear, the cold damp morning air crept into my bones causing an involuntary shiver, but it wasn't just the cold and dampness giving me goose pimples. The place seemed to have a sinister atmosphere about it. I couldn't quite put my finger on it, but it just didn't feel comfortable. Eventually my preoccupation with the cold and feeling of discomfort with the place was interrupted by Rob Taylor as he wandered over followed by a couple of officers and Ian Briggs. Ian, pointing to a small hilly patch of woodland explained that was where the baiting had taken place followed by a request to follow him. As we made our way through the rough sheep grazed pasture to cross a narrow plank bridge over the stream I paused briefly to take in my surroundings.

The low misty cloud was now beginning to drift away to reveal the steep rugged slopes of the hills above. The twisted, stunted forms of mountain ash and oak stood out like ancient sentinels amongst dense thickets of common gorse, now drab and flowerless on this February morning. In spring their coconut scented bright yellow flowers would add a blaze of cheerful colour to the bleakness of the stone crags and spoil heaps of grey slate. Eventually we arrived at a metal farm gate leading into the wood and the location of the covertly filmed badger baiting and where I would begin my work.

I immediately saw what appeared to be pipes protruding out of the wooded hillside set amongst a number of large paving slabs. Further investigation quickly revealed that the pipes were in fact buried flexible plastic land drainage pipes of around thirty centimetres in diameter leading to a series of small artificial chambers constructed from thick round plastic tubs around fifty centimetres in diameter and sixty centimetres in height with a solid floor and a roof consisting of the large heavy paving slabs. A hole had been cut into the sides of the tubs in order to attach the pipes which led from the chamber to exit into the woodland. Large heavy stones lay close by to block the pipe entrances to prevent any animal unfortunate enough to be a prisoner in this labyrinth of pipes and chambers from escaping.

Upon immediately discovering badger hair by the first pipe, I made my way to a stone paving slab a few metres away which, when removed, revealed an artificial chamber containing both badger and fox hair in the leaf litter of the floor. And so, it went on from chamber to chamber each connected to a pipe leading out to the wood. I sketched out the area indicating the position of all the pipes and chambers and where evidence of badger and fox had been discovered. Individual numbered markers were placed at strategic evidential points, photographed, logged and location indicated on my sketch of the area. The hair of badger and fox along with skulls and any other removal evidence were logged, photographed, and placed in evidence bags.

With my examination of the pipes and chambers complete I next began an examination of the woodland boundary looking for evidence of badger and fox in the form of well used paths, signs of the animals passing under fences, hair, scats, and any other indication that either species were routinely passing through the wood naturally.

I found no evidence to indicate that either species were entering the wood of their own volition indicating that evidence of badger and fox discovered in the pipes and chambers led to the assumption that the animal had been placed there involuntarily rather than of their own accord. The only evidence I found of either species in the area other than the pipes or chambers was in the form of skeletal remains, strongly indicating that a number of individuals from both species had in fact died there and been left to rot.

I could come to no other conclusion that the network of pipes and chambers had been constructed for no other reason than to hold captive a badger and fox until the farmer come Dwyryd hunt master and his cronies got the urge once more to feed their cruel sadistic cravings by baiting one or the other with dogs. To do this they would remove the boulder used to block the pipe entrance, followed by removing the stone slab to reveal a terrified animal hiding in the darkness of the chamber. At this point, the badger or fox would be prodded and poked until it made a dash down the now open pipe in the hope of escape from its tormentor. Sadly, as soon it emerged, it wasn't the sweet smell of freedom that awaited it but the sadistically cruel morons waiting to unleash their dogs to pursue, savage and eventually rip it to shreds.

These pathetic excuses for human beings revelled in this debauchery to the extent that every so often they would pull the dogs off only to release them again when the now totally exhausted and injured animal made a feeble and desperate attempt at escape. In all probability the foxes would have been used to train young dogs to bait and kill without the danger of them being injured. The fox is a slight animal compared to the much heavier and stronger badger who, when given no other alternative but to fight, will use every ounce of his strength and agility combined with his powerful bite and dogged determination to see off his tormentors.

Under normal circumstances the badger is a shy inoffensive creature who asks for nothing more than to be left alone and quietly go about his business, and if given the choice of fight or flight will choose the latter every time. But take fleeing out of the equation and he will fight a terribly ferocious battle with dogs being ragged and severely injured, often with jaws almost ripped off. Woefully it's the badger's power and tenacity that makes him the object of the badger diggers and baiters sadistic pleasures. They go to enormous lengths to dig him out of his sett where they will either kill him or take him away to be baited in a pit by an untold number of dogs from terriers and lurchers to bull terriers, with bets placed on whose dog will fare the best. But this Dwyryd hunt master going by the by the name of David Thomas and his cronies were merely encouraging their dogs to savage an animal for no other reason than to satisfy their cruel sadistic cravings.

After a few hours of examining the scene and gathering evidence I finally concluded my investigation and headed back to the farm whereupon I was asked to hang around in case anything else cropped up that may warrant my presence. Not that I could have gone anywhere anyway as my policeman taxi driver was there for the duration!

I decided to make the most of my free time by grabbing a brew and munching on a sandwich and as I did so, Rob and other officers were busy removing a variety of firearms from the farmhouse and loading them in the boot of a police car whilst the farmer-come-Dwyryd-hunt master voiced his objections. RSPCA Inspectors were materializing from all corners of the farm with what appeared to be a never-ending stream of terriers and lurchers to be confiscated. This in itself was a time-consuming operation as each one had to be examined by a vet and recorded before being loaded into one of the many RSPCA vans. Each and every one of the dogs were discovered living in shockingly squalid conditions. Jack Russell and Patterdale terriers were discovered on chain leashes attached to a stake in steep field corners with nothing more than a filthy plastic barrel to crawl into to offer some respite from the cold and wet with filthy food and water dishes lying empty amongst disgusting mounds of faeces. Other dogs were kept in small steel cages, the doors of which were securely locked with heavy duty padlocks. For whatever reason, no key was forthcoming and as such the firearms unit were requested to attend with their powerful bolt cutters in order that those dogs could also be taken away.

I was in the process of putting my flask and now empty butty box back into my rucksack when I was asked to take a look at a couple of empty cages in an old stone building across the farmyard. As I made my way there, I passed RSPCA Inspectors toing and froing from fields to vans and back again as they retrieved more dogs. Hounds bayed loudly as they stood on their hind legs to peer through the bars of the hunt kennels in eager anticipation of either food, exercise, or a hunt.

Eventually a voice cried, "In here Malcolm," from an open door. Upon entering I was asked to examine a couple of disgustingly filthy blood-stained wire cages containing the remains of half-eaten pheasants. It was obvious that they had been used to contain an animal and a more detailed examination revealed fox hair. This led to no other conclusion other than the cages had been used to hold a fox or foxes and from what I had seen in the wood I think it a reasonable assumption to assume that the poor creatures had been thrown to the dogs.

I had just finished taking photographs of the cages and bagging fox hair as evidence when I was asked to take a look at a second cage discovered in an old stone cattle shed. As I followed the Inspector we passed through dark narrow alleyways between buildings when we came across a half barrel shaped metal contraption on legs holding a dead sheep. It had been placed on its back and had its throat cut. Presumably, the animal was deemed as being beyond any commercial value and as such was destined as food for the hounds. A disgusting sight! The only description fitting the place was an animal's equivalent of hell! But there was more to come!

We finally arrived at a long stone building and as we passed through an open cobwebbed door my sense of smell went into overload as a disgusting concoction of odours from dog poo to fox and the stench of decaying meat emitting from an open topped 45-gallon drum hit my senses. The place was dismal with only a shadowy light coming from an open door at the far end and a few small cobwebbed encrusted windows allowing a narrow gleam of light to enter.

The sound of wailing and barking of dogs coming from somewhere within only added to the dreadful atmosphere. I paused for a minute or two to allow my senses to adjust to the stench and gloom. Eventually the Inspector asked me to follow her to the far end of the building towards the shadowy light. As I followed, I discovered where the location of the barking and whining of dogs was coming from. It was a small dark room with a doorless entrance, as I peeked in, I was met by a putrid disgusting smell along with the excited high-pitched yelps of dogs and the rattling of chains. As my eyes adjusted to the gloom, I saw four lurcher type dogs, each with a chain dangling from their collar attached to the wall. As they lunged forward the chains rattled and clinked until they reached their limit whereupon the dogs came to a sudden halt as the chain viciously tugged at their necks to yank them sharply back. The floor must have been a foot deep in faeces and like the terriers in the field, dirty, empty food and water bowls lay scattered amongst the filth.

The dogs weren't aggressive, the barking, whining and lunging was purely in eager anticipation of the possibility of being taken out. Sadly, not to be fussed over or taken a walk, but to hunt or to rip a fox or badger to death.

This wasn't the dogs fault; they were hunters by nature and this sad life was all they knew. Affection was something these poor creatures had probably never experienced; they were as much a victim of cruelty as were the badgers and foxes they were encouraged to savage.

Eventually I stole myself away from that hell hole to arrive at the far end of the building and the cage. What a sorry sad sight it was! A petrified fox lay in a corner of the cage whilst less than a metre away a constantly barking terrier dog was chained to the wall. At first, I thought the fox was dead, but it wasn't, it was paralysed with fear! The four lurchers chained to the wall were rescued along with the fox. Sadly, the vet decided that due to its suffering and appalling condition the kindest end was euthanasia.

How the hell can people be so indifferently and shockingly cruel? I've rescued foxes, hand-reared orphaned cubs, rehabilitated foxes, studied foxes and for over ten years had the pleasure of the company of two tame, rescued foxes, Muffles and Velvet. And believe you me, foxes are truly sentient beings with emotions. They feel pleasure, they feel pain, and they are intelligent and playful. My own two displayed all of those and more including genuine affection.

Finally, it was over. It had been a very long and stressful day albeit a productive one.

But definitely a day of mixed emotions. Sadness for the foxes and badgers that for God knows how long had endured horrendous, barbaric cruelty, and joy for the dogs that had at last been freed from that hell hole.

The only dogs not to be taken were a working sheep dog and the hunt hounds due to them at least seeming to be living in reasonable conditions.

It was quite late when the police car finally dropped me off at the bottom of the track and, as I wearily made my way up to the house, I couldn't wait to run a hot bath and wash away the stench of the place.

A few days later I got around to the task of sorting out my notes and photographs in order to begin compiling my report. Once done and mulled over a few times to ensure I hadn't missed anything I submitted it to the RSPCA who were taking the prosecution. Eventually a trial date was set for the 5th February 2018 over a period of three days at Llandudno Magistrates Court, presided over by a district judge with me being called as expert witness for the prosecution with regards to badger baiting offences. The defence consisted of three lawyers, one of whom was my old adversary from way back with Leemax, the hunting vet, as their expert witness.

The role of an expert witness is to be totally impartial with the sole purpose of assisting the court with regards to various aspects of the case. Now that sounds fine on paper but in reality, the defence will try everything in the book to twist the truth to their advantage and if they don't like your answer to a particular question then be prepared for a session of head slapping cross examination! And boy, have I had some head slapping!!

On the second day of the trial, I was called to the stand. The first defence lawyer to question me was my old adversary from way back who just did his job without malice and didn't give me too much of a hard time. But the others certainly made up for it!!

One in particular pushed the boundaries to its limits with his intense and aggressive cross examination to the extent that the prosecution objected on a couple of occasions with even the judge intervening. But undeterred he continued pushing in his quest to wear me down. At one point he fired a question at me which I didn't see the logic behind and returned with a question of my own. That really wound him up and looking as though his blood pressure was about to go through the roof, he aggressively informed me that he was the one asking the questions, not me!! After yet another objection from the prosecution plus a reprimand from the judge he rephrased the original question. Before giving him the satisfaction of immediately answering I looked at the judge who nodded indicating that yes, I should answer the question.

Their aim is to put you under as much pressure as they think they can get away with in the hope that you become flustered and give them an opportunity to gain the upper hand. One sign of weakness and they are in there like a pack of African hunting dogs!

Eventually my cross examination came to an end and the judge called a one hour break for lunch and I was able to relax a little. Just prior to reconvening the prosecution lawyer took me into a side room and asked me to look at a few A4 copies of photographs about to be offered as defence evidence. These had purportedly been taken by Leemax at the scene of the baiting, but they were in total contradiction to my own. I had no hesitation in advising that they were most certainly not taken at the same location and that the defence were obviously trying it on.

A few minutes later the call came that the court was about to reconvene and could everyone take their seats. A few minutes later the call came to all rise as the judge entered followed by the call for Leemax as the defence expert witness to take the stand.

He rose from his seat and strode confidently to the witness box where he gave the oath followed by being given the choice of sitting or standing to deliver his evidence whereupon he chose the former. The defence lawyers put their various opening questions to him which he answered in his usual self-confident manner whilst lounging casually in his seat as if in his living room watching TV.

After the defence had finished it was the turn of the prosecution who, now armed with the dodgy photographs, went in nice and slowly to begin with giving Leemax a sense of false security. And then bang!! The photos were produced and one by one handed to Leemax with a request that he explain what they were depicting and where they were taken.

At this point he rose from his seat and, with visibly shaking hands, attempted to convince the court that they had been taken at the scene in question and that his were true and mine were not. Eventually the judge asked that if handed an ordnance survey map could he point out the area in question.

He stuttered that he would attempt to do so but in reality, he found the task rather difficult.

The judge put more questions to him with the final one being, "Mr Leemax, did you actually take these photographs?"

He paused for a few moments before finally admitting that he had not!

The judge responded with the obvious question of, "Well Mr Leemax, if you didn't take them who did?"

More hesitation before he blurted out, "Mr Thomas took them!"

The flabbergasted judge replied with, "You mean to tell me that Mr Thomas, the defendant, took the pictures?!"

At this point Leemax had well and truly lost his air of self-confidence, along with the smug smile, as he stuttered that on arrival at the farm and hunt kennels, he realised that the batteries were flat on his camera and that Mr Thomas had kindly offered to take the photographs for him on his mobile phone.

To say that the judge was gobsmacked would be an understatement! He couldn't believe the audacity, not to mention the dishonesty of his actions and gave him a lecture on the seriousness of his actions before releasing him from the stand. Needless to say, his report was dismissed as false.

Leemax's one and only visit to the site was some months after the raid and my examination whereupon the defendant Thomas ferried him around on a quad bike and apparently showed him where the photographs needed to be taken which plainly wasn't at the scene of the baiting.

After Leemax's so called evidence, the covertly filmed badger baiting footage was shown on the courtroom's large TV screen along with an explanation as to exactly what was happening. To say it was distressing to watch would be an understatement!

How people can inflict such terrible suffering on an animal is totally beyond my comprehension! These people are rotten to the core and would not think twice about inflicting the same suffering on you or me if they thought they could get away with it.

On the morning of day three, the final day of the trial, the vet gave his expert opinion with regards to the condition of the dogs and foxes, after which the defence and prosecution gave their closing arguments to the court prior to the judge's deliberations.

The judge retired to chamber to consider the case, returning an hour later to deliver a verdict of guilty of all charges and handed out the following sentences.

The defendants -

David W Thomas aged 55 and Hunt Master of the Dwyryd Fox Hounds for thirty-two years was imprisoned for twenty-two weeks and placed under close supervision for a period of twelve months. He also had to pay costs totalling £5,000 and disqualified from keeping dogs for eight years.

Jordan A. Houlston aged 24 was imprisoned for twenty weeks and placed under a supervision order for a period of twelve months. He was ordered to pay costs of £600, a victim surcharge of £150 and disqualified from keeping dogs for eight years.

Mark W. Morris aged 26 was given a ten-week prison sentence suspended for twelve months. Ordered to pay £500 in costs plus £150 surcharge. He also received a four-year disqualification from keeping dogs.

A 17-year-old youth was handed a ten-month referral order, a four-year ban on keeping dogs plus £200 costs and a £20 surcharge.

At the end of the trial, RSPCA Chief Inspector Briggs of the Special Ops Unit stated, "This was a major landmark investigation in which the RSPCA had caught a number of individuals red handed in the act of using dogs to barbarically fight with badger."

And just to prove how determined these people are to continue in their barbaric activities, on the 7th November 2022 following another covert surveillance operation, this time by the League Against Cruel Sports, the police and RSPCA once again raided the Dwyryd hunt kennels and farm resulting in Thomas, still the Hunt Master of the Dwyryd Fox Hounds, finding himself once again in Llandudno Magistrates Court awaiting sentence for offences under the Animal Welfare Act along with his 18 year old son. Ironically, he faced the same district judge who presided over the badger baiting case in 2018.

Despite being given an eight-year ban from keeping dogs in 2018, he was charged with failing to provide for the needs of twenty-nine dogs and 2 ferrets. He received a twenty-four-week custodial sentence for offences under the Animal Welfare Act and breaching his eight year ban on keeping dogs. He was also given a further ten-year disqualification on keeping dogs. His son was ordered to carry out 160 hours unpaid work, £600 costs and also received a ten-year ban on keeping dogs.

In total the RSPCA took away a total of twenty-eight surviving dogs, including the fox hounds and two ferrets. One of the dogs also had injuries consistent with having been in a fight with a badger. Surprise, surprise!!

A week after the trial, Thomas lodged an appeal heard at Mold Crown Court in Flintshire, North Wales, resulting in a judge sitting with a bench of magistrates reducing his sentence to thirteen weeks suspended for twelve months and ordered his immediate release from prison. At least the court costs remained plus the ban on keeping dogs but if his past history is anything to go by, he will carry on regardless. Individuals like him have no regard for any creature. Cruelty is so embedded in their DNA that they will never stop.

Unfortunately, this wouldn't be the end of my dealings with badger diggers and baiters, as the years to follow would see me becoming more embroiled in the investigation of their heinous crimes.

9

BBC Wales Investigates 'The Secret World Of Badger Baiters'

The Dwyryd Hunt badger baiting trial created a fair amount of media attention with both local and national newspapers reporting on the story, plus TV coverage. BBC Wales in particular covered the case in detail, with a reporter and camera crew outside Llandudno Magistrates Court on a daily basis capturing Thomas and his cronies arriving in the morning. Thomas made a pathetic sight as he scurried past the reporters and TV cameras with a Tesco shopping bag over his head trying to pay no heed to the constant calls from the posse of reporters vying for a comment. His little entourage consisted of his wife, co-defendants and one or two of his cronies scampering alongside him. His wife looked tense and uncomfortable in total contrast to the others who gave two fingers to the cameras whilst screaming expletives. Their only respite from the onslaught came as they dashed through the main door of the court building and passed through security. Obviously, the cameras were not allowed to follow but being undeterred, they patiently waited outside for their prey to exit at the end of the day.

I usually arrived at court around 9.30am with the first task being the daily routine of security checks entailing emptying the contents of your pockets into a plastic tray followed by bags, briefcase or whatever else you may have with you being thoroughly inspected and rummaged through. Next you proceed through the body scanner and so long as it doesn't blow a gasket whilst emitting ear piercing bleeps you are allowed to retrieve anything not temporarily confiscated. Then and only then are you allowed into the inner sanctum of the building.

Now, this is my nemesis! Whether it be in a court building or an airport you can virtually guarantee that I will fail at least one of these routine checks and heave a huge sigh of relief if I pass through unscathed. Some years ago, in Nairobi airport I had three attempts at succeeding until finally the exasperated security lady having discovered no explanation for the alert allowed me to continue my journey.

Thankfully, the body scanner in Llandudno Magistrates Court must have taken a shine to me and allowed me to pass through without emitting a single bleep. After retrieving loose change, wallet, and other miscellaneous items from the tray I climbed the stairs to the public waiting area and courts 1 and 2. Everyone, including the defendants and their entourage would be hanging around here to await the start of the day's proceedings. Thomas's wife would greet me with a nervous smile and a good morning whilst during lunch break or other recess his brother-in-law would endeavour to engage me in conversation. I found their mentality very strange to say the least and couldn't help but ponder over the thought that perhaps the penny hadn't dropped that I was the expert witness for the prosecution. But of course, they were fully aware of that fact and any pleasantries from them were more than made up for by the defendant's arrogance and swagger, coupled with their occasional sniggers and snide remarks.

They would sit in the defendant's box listening to the proceedings and watching the covertly filmed footage of their badger baiting as it played on the court's screen, showing not the slightest hint of emotion or remorse. On the contrary, on occasions they even seemed to find it amusing and let out an occasional snigger. But as mentioned in the previous chapter the judge's verdict and sentence soon wiped the smiles off their faces as they were led down to the cells and the awaiting G4S prison van to escort them to their new lodgings at what was then Her Majesty's pleasure.

Immediately after the David Thomas trial I was approached by BBC Wales who explained that they were in the final stages of putting together a documentary called 'The Secret World of Badger Baiters' and could I possibly help with a bit of filming? The producer went on to explain that for the past six months, they had employed the services of an ex-military guy, now working as an undercover journalist going under the pseudonym of John to infiltrate a gang of illegal hunters and badger baiters. These guys apparently travelled far and wide to satisfy their lust for sadistic cruelty to any animal that took their fancy. Unfortunately for them they were totally oblivious to the fact that one of their gangs was secretly filming everything on two tiny cameras, one concealed in a coat and the other in a shirt.

The cameras had filmed hours upon hours of sickening footage of animals being hunted and barbarically killed. Some of the most horrific showed them attempting to kill a deer in the Forest of Dean, allowing dogs to savage a wild boar before stabbing it with a knife and the sickening spectacle of them torturing a badger cub before killing it with a spade. BBC Wales were hoping to include footage of badgers not fighting for their lives but doing nothing more than peacefully going about their business, which of course was in total contrast to the main content of the documentary that also included badger baiting footage from my previous case at the Dwyryd Hunt kennels and farm.

It just so happened that we had badgers wandering through the garden in search of their nightly treat of peanuts scattered on the drive and directly below the conservatory. These badgers were totally at ease and quite accustomed to the area being illuminated plus being gawked at from the confines of the conservatory. I explained this to the producer resulting in a camera crew, accompanied by BBC journalist and presenter Wyre Davies spending a few hours guzzling copious amounts of tea and coffee and dunking digestive biscuits whilst filming badgers contentedly munching away on peanuts.

The programme was finally televised on 22nd May 2018, after which the BBC passed the footage from the two concealed cameras along with other relevant evidence over to the RSPCA. On 15th August 2018, they asked if I could view the footage, now referred to as IM/9 Dig Shirt Cam and Dig Coat Cam and compile a report regarding my conclusions. To say that the viewing was difficult would be an understatement. I thought the badger baiting footage from the hunt kennels in Blaenau Ffestiniog was bad, but this was worse in the respect that it also contained the horrific cruelty inflicted upon the deer, wild boar, and the badger cub.

Even after all my years of doing this kind of work my blood still boils with anger when watching these things; but I can't allow my personal feelings to cloud my judgment. My priority is to remain completely unbiased in my conclusions with my report stating nothing but the facts. If a case ultimately goes to court my job as expert witness is to assist and advise the court in a totally objective and unbiased manner, regardless of whom I may be representing as an expert.

The footage left no doubt in my mind as to what was taking place despite the fact that no badger was actually seen in the footage. However, my report stated that the individuals depicted in the footage were knowingly digging an active badger sett followed by the reasons for my conclusions.

The footage clearly showed them spending many hours *(ten in total!)* digging deep into what was clearly a badger sett with yapping terriers being transported by the scruff of the neck from one section of the sett to another. First in the field then over the fence and down a steep wooded bank leading down to a river. Dogs wearing transmitter collars were put into various holes where they would work their way through the labyrinth of tunnels and chambers in their task to locate a badger. A typical scenario in these situations is when a terrier comes across his quarry he will begin to bay or bark - or to give tongue, as the diggers call it - and will in all probability be deep within the maze of tunnels and chambers as he faces a standoff against the badger. The diggers above ground put their ears to the sett entrances as they hear the distant baying listening for other sounds to give them an idea as to what may be taking place deep within.

Once fairly certain that the terrier is baying at a badger, they will use a small portable receiver to pinpoint the exact location of the dog via its transmitter collar and the dig begins! Suddenly the air is filled with the crash of spades entering the earth coupled with the excited barks and yelps of dogs not yet employed in the hunt, intermingled with the curses, and swearing of the diggers. This is hard toil and before long jackets are discarded to hang off a fence or thrown in a heap on the ground. Beads of sweat trickle down their backs as they dig deeper and deeper into the set. The baying of the terrier gets fainter as both dog and badger travel deeper and deeper. Every now and again they will take a breather from their labours to wipe away the sweat, smoke a cigarette and down a can of beer or two to quench their thirst. Once refreshed they will walk around the general area of the sett and with receiver in hand attempt to relocate the terrier. Eventually it bursts into life giving a strong signal from below and the relentless digging begins once more.

The hours roll by, and the digging continues amidst more cursing, sweating, smoking, and downing of beers. By now the scene is reminiscent of a mini battlefield with holes plummeting vertically deep into the earth with mounds of excavated soil scattered around like giant mole hills intermingled amongst discarded cigarette butts and beer cans.

Every once in while the air will become tense and filled with even more rowdily uttered expletives as they catch a glimpse of their quarry. The dogs above ground some of which had taken their turn in the hunt run around yapping in excited anticipation, their wiry coats matted with soil and blood. One or two may have suffered terrible injuries with jaws almost ripped off but too full of adrenalin to feel the pain, whilst others bark and whine as they pull and tug on their leashes tethered to a fence or stake eager to play their part in the hunt.

At the end of the day the typical outcome of this barbarity will be badly injured dogs and badgers who, like their canine adversaries, are covered in dirt and blood. The badger is dragged from his home to be hideously killed either by the blows of a spade or, if these subhumans wish to prolong their sadistic pleasures, he will be thrown to the ground and a chance to flee.

But it's merely a ploy and after a few brief moments of liberty they will let loose the bigger more powerful dogs in the form of lurchers or bull terrier types to chase and set upon him once more. I have even seen footage of them taking pot shots at a fleeing badger with a shotgun.

Sadly, whatever they choose, old Brock is dead!

None of this is pleasant reading but it is the reality of badger digging and baiting and describes in some small way the mentality of the people involved.

Once the programme had aired and they had received notices of prosecution they were now fully aware that one of their gang was an undercover journalist who had captured all of their sadistic cruelty on film, they still insisted in their defence that they were oblivious to the fact that they were digging a badger sett and were merely after fox.

To counteract this, the covertly filmed footage also records their conversations where they can clearly be heard referring to their quarry as 'pig.' *(Pig being a common term for badgers used by badger diggers and baiters)* In their defence, these individuals often claim they were after fox or merely out rabbiting and totally unaware that they were digging a badger sett. How they can claim this to be a believable defence is beyond comprehension, particularly when the evidence clearly proves otherwise. I can only assume that not only are they unbelievably cruel and sadistic but also extremely thick! But thick or not, in court their defence will try every trick in the book to convince all and sundry that their clients are as pure as the driven snow.

Shortly after viewing the footage and submitting my report, the RSPCA asked me to travel down to the village of Llanddewi Velfrey, Pembrokeshire in Southwest Wales to visit the location of the covertly filmed badger dig. Despite the fact that a fair amount of time had passed they thought it worthwhile I examine the area to determine if the sett was in fact still active and to gather any evidence to determine the fact. I was also tasked with recording any remaining evidence of the dig that may be present and to submit a second report of my findings and conclusions. Up to this point the only evidence had been the covertly filmed footage which was very much self-explanatory in that they were filmed spending many hours digging in a field and wood accompanied by dogs. They were frequently heard to use the word 'pig' with regards to their quarry but no badger, dead or otherwise was actually filmed and no one had actually examined the location.

Once I have completed an investigation into an incident of wildlife crime, my report can often be the deciding factor on whether or not the incident proceeds to trial. The investigation has to be as thorough as it possibly can be, with all evidence, no matter how small or insignificant it may seem at the time, collated and recorded in preparation for the most time-consuming task of all, putting it all together in an easily readable and understood report.

On the 24th August 2018, I set off bright and early to begin the long drive down to the location. The journey was pretty much uneventful, apart from when approaching a field bordered by a patch a woodland, I spotted a good number of red kites soaring gracefully above the treetops, their reddish-brown plumage, angled wings and deeply forked tail making them unmistakable. Despite being on a fairly tight schedule, I couldn't resist the temptation to pull over for a few moments to enjoy the spectacle and reflect on the fact that after some three hundred years of relentless persecution they were literally on the brink of extinction as a UK species destined to follow in the footsteps of the European beaver, wolf and bear.

It's ironical that in medieval times particularly in the city of London the red kite, due to their scavenging habits, was a protected species and regarded as an invaluable street cleaner. Thankfully, due to various reintroduction schemes in the late 1980s and early 1990s to bolster the last remaining remnants of the population in Wales, their numbers slowly began to recover. It was literally clawed back from the precipice of eradication. Thankfully now many years later it is a common sight in most of its former stronghold and beyond. At the present time of 2023, the red kite comeback is a complete success story and particularly so here in Wales.

But as much as I was relishing the spectacle I still had a few miles to cover before reaching my destination and, as such, reluctantly continued my journey deeper into rural South Wales. A couple of hours later I pulled into a farmyard to meet up with an RSPCA Inspector from the Special Ops Team who, after introducing me to the farmer, pointed in the direction of a line of trees a couple of fields away, explaining that was the location of the covertly filmed badger digging followed by a request to grab my gear and follow him to the spot.

The fields were large and gently dropping away towards the line of trees, eventually leaving the farm out of view as it dipped below the horizon. As we got closer, I began to recognise the location from the video footage with the wood and field separated by a fence and a few other familiar landmarks. My eyes were immediately drawn to a spot in the field close to the fence line where a number of areas roughly a metre square appeared to have been dug then backfilled with the turf replaced in a crude attempt to conceal evidence that any digging had taken place. Further signs of disturbance in the form of fairly deep depressions with compacted and sparsely vegetated soil lay scattered beyond the backfilled and re turfed areas.

Despite the time scale between the digging incident and my visit, evidence was still easily visible, as were signs of current badger activity. My first task was to make a sketch of the field area noting down areas of interest. Whilst doing this I followed a well-worn badger path from the field to the fence. The path continued under the fence to enter a steep wooded area dropping down to the river Taf. Tufts of coarse black and white badger outer guard hairs around nine to ten centimetres in length hung from the bottom strand of barbed wire where it had been snatched from their backs as they passed under the fence. I plucked a few hairs from the clump which, when rolled between thumb and forefinger, felt fresh and pliable with the distinct oval shape known as elliptical.

Before continuing over the fence into the steep woodland, I began to concentrate my examination in the field. I placed numbered evidence markers by any areas displaying signs of human disturbance in the form of digging etc., with their positions indicated on my sketch. I then proceeded to photograph the numbered evidence and take notes with regards to the type of evidence found i.e. signs of human disturbance, badger hair (*photographed in situ before being bagged as evidence*) badger paths and footprints (*badger or otherwise*) Basically I noted anything that could potentially be classified as evidence of human disturbance and of past and current badger activity. It's also important to note here that I will also document any evidence of fox or rabbit as signs of both species can be found in or around a currently active sett.

Once satisfied that I had fully examined and documented the field I then climbed over the fence to repeat the process in the wooded area. I was dismayed to discover that the wood was being used as a convenient dumping ground for a variety of farm associated rubbish with plastic animal feed bags, tin cans, bailing twine and rusting barbed wire scattered amongst the trees and rocks. It was so sad that what should have been a beautiful piece of woodland dropping steeply down to the river Taf was being treated as nothing more than the farms rubbish tip. How people can have such total disregard for the environment and its associated wildlife is completely beyond my comprehension!

As with the field above, I soon discovered evidence of badger sett disturbance, both historical and recent, along with other undisturbed sett entrances consistent with those of badger. These were in the classic shape of an inverted D measuring approximately thirty centimetres by thirty centimetres with mounds of excavated spoil and displaying signs of current badger activity. I also collected badger hair and discovered fresh footprints displaying the typical broad five toed pads and long claws typical of badger along with fresh latrines. Despite the time gap between the badger digging gang having been on the site and my examination, I was able to confirm that the sett, despite showing obvious signs of historical and relatively recent human disturbance, was a currently active, well established main sett. My findings left me with no reason to believe that it was no different at the time of the digging. The following day upon my return home, I began the time-consuming task of making sense of my findings by marrying up my sketch, notes, and photos in preparation for compiling my report.

Finally, after many hours the report was finished and ready for submitting to the RSPCA for their legal team's perusal. Court cases are very expensive affairs, and the prosecution needs to be fairly confident of a positive result before committing a case to trial, hence so much relying on the accuracy of my investigation and the quality of the report. If the prosecution deems either to be flawed, they won't wish to gamble on a costly negative result and as a result a gang of badger baiters walk free. Get it right, and the chances of a guilty verdict are in your favour. But in this game, nothing is guaranteed! Despite what may appear to be a rock-solid case the defence will be like a lrabid dog with a bone to prove otherwise. Eventually I received notification that the case was to be heard over four days at Cardiff Crown Court starting on 30 September 2019 and presided over by a district judge.

My wife Ann and I booked into the conveniently situated Angel Hotel in the city centre, opposite the magnificent medieval Cardiff Castle and a short ten-minute stroll to the Crown Court. It was a long drive from our little rural hideaway in North Wales down to the metropolis of the Welsh capital and we were both a little weary by the time we entered the hustle and bustle of Cardiff's city traffic. As we were approaching the castle on our right, we spotted the road on our left that would have taken us to the hotel car park but, sods law, it was closed off for road works!! Now being unfamiliar with the intricacies of Cardiff's traffic system we had no choice but to drive by until we could pull over and check the street map for an alternative route.

Thankfully, it wasn't too much of a detour and we were soon parked up and checking in. After a quick freshen up and arranging our various items of clothing on hangers we made our way down to the dining room for a much-needed evening meal. With appetites fulfilled the remainder of the evening was spent in the room relaxing. Ann read a book whilst I poured myself a Scotch and plonked myself down by the large window overlooking the street and the castle entrance below. The scene was quite surreal, with the castle and its impressive Victorian Clock tower, designed by William Burges in 1866, now illuminated, casting shimmering lights through the evenings drizzle to reflect off the damp busy road below. Eventually I retrieved my prosecution report from my suitcase with every intention of going through it one last time, but you can only do so much. My mind was becoming jumbled and after some thirty minutes or, so it was cast aside to leave me with my thoughts of what the following few days had in store.

Despite all my years of attending court to give expert evidence you can guarantee that the night before a case my mind will be spinning with a multitude of thoughts resulting in the possibility of good night's sleep being a bit of a hit and miss affair. But sleep or no sleep I needed to be up bright and early and as such stumbled out of bed at 6.30am the following morning. I drew the curtains back, the half-light of dawn strengthened by the still glowing streetlights filtered through the window. I wandered over to the tea and coffee making facilities to top up my caffeine levels before heading off to the bathroom for my morning ablutions. With caffeine levels and ablutions out of the way we wandered down to the dining room for a leisurely breakfast and to mentally prepare myself for the day's proceedings in the knowledge that at some point during of the course of the trial I would be called to give evidence and face the inevitable cross examination from the team defence lawyers.

With breakfast over and done with we made our way back to the room where I changed from my casual breakfast wear into the more formal court attire of suit and tie. After a final check to ensure that I had everything - mobile phone, cash to purchase refreshments and, of course, the all-important report, off we went. The proceedings were due to start at 10 am but court timetables are notoriously fickle with delays commonplace. But despite the uncertainty of such things, it's always advisable to arrive early to allow time for the formalities of security checks. There is nothing more stressful than arriving at the last minute and having to wait your turn at the security desk due to the person in front producing everything from coins of the realm to a half-eaten sandwich from every possible orifice as if they were auditioning for the role of court magician. Then when you think they have finished, and the plastic contents tray is overflowing they pass through the body scanner for the damn thing to start bleeping whereupon the process of checking pockets and bags etc. starts all over again!!

Anyway, in an effort to try and avoid any unnecessary delays, we left the hotel around 9 am to embark on the short stroll to the court. After side stepping the hustle and bustle of morning traffic and dashing pedestrians, we arrived at the Cathays Park area of the city and the grade I listed Victorian building of Cardiff Crown Court. And what an impressive building it is with its imposing dome topped turrets gazing down upon a flight of Portland stone steps flanked by lampstands surmounted by dragons. As we passed through the large heavy oak double doors into the main entrance lobby, we were met with the usual security preliminaries which thankfully we sailed through.

With security checks over and the contents of our pockets retrieved we ascended a rather grand wide oak stairway opening out into a large public area with oak panelling adorning the walls, topped by a high ornate ceiling and marble fireplaces. At each end corridors led into witness waiting rooms, lawyers briefing rooms and heavy large oak doors taking you into the inner sanctum of one of the nine courtrooms. All very grand and in complete contrast to some of the totally characterless court buildings I've frequented over the years with Birkenhead and Wallasey magistrates courts on the Wirral springing to mind. I recently googled Wirral courts and wasn't in the least surprised to find a list of reviews with a lowly figure of two out of five. You can just imagine a couple of disgruntled defendants having been in the dock saying, 'I'm not coming here again, they've just given me 200 hours community service plus court costs!! If they think I'm giving them a good review they can think again!'

Anyway, back to Cardiff!

As there didn't appear to be anyone else around involved in the case we got ourselves a coffee from a vending machine that somehow didn't quite fit in with the Victorian splendour of its surroundings. We sat ourselves down on one of the many benches and seats scattered around the place to await the day's proceedings.

As I sat there sipping my nondescript tepid latte I marvelled at the grandeur of the place. It exuded an atmosphere of being in the inner sanctum of the judicial chambers of law with wigged barristers in their flowing gowns purposely striding up and down. Some in deep conversation with another whilst others gave the impression of urgency as they dashed around clutching a maroon cardboard coffee cup in one hand, the contents of which sloshed around like a bucket of water on a trampoline, whilst clutching at a pile of pink ribbon bound papers precariously tucked under the opposing arm.

I have been in numerous courts from Magistrates to Crown, and as mentioned before many are pretty mediocre affairs that would struggle to win any architectural prizes, but Cardiff Crown Court was certainly the exception. Nevertheless, I wasn't there to merely sit around admiring the architectural delights of the building or eye balling the diversity of people dashing to and fro. But nonetheless it was an interesting exercise. From the barristers in their wigs and flowing gowns, to suited individuals, who presumably hoped that their appearance of respectability would be a positive influence on the court. At totally the opposite end of the spectrum were those who gave the impression of having had just climbed out of bed and thrown on whatever item of clothing was at hand. Some in tatty jeans and T shirt sporting tattoos from head to toe who, with a swaggering air of bravado strived to give a casual couldn't care less attitude. I couldn't help but ponder over who these faceless people were and why were they there? Were they like myself, there to give evidence or were they destined for the dock? What was their story? People watching can be an intriguing pastime!

But I was well aware as to why I was there, and it wasn't long before my people watching came to an abrupt end with the arrival of the RSPCA's prosecution lawyer to escort me away. As I followed him to a tiny side room, I couldn't help but notice a rather large rotund elderly chap who, despite his large size, his suit appeared to hang off him.

He was sat on a bench talking to a woman and as I passed by, I heard him remark, "Don't worry, once I get him up there, he'll know about it!!"

I remember thinking at the time blimey he means business! I wonder who he's going to be brutalising under cross examination?!

At 10 am sharp court security arrived to unlock the door to court three allowing a throng, from lawyers to press and members of the public to enter. My wife Ann grabbed a front row seat in the public area at the back of the room whilst other interested parties, from family members and friends of the defendant to a Hunt Sab or two jostled for a seat. It was pretty obvious which particular side people represented by their voluntary segregation amidst furtive glances and whispers. Some remained a mystery not appearing to be associated with either side and provoked some speculation from both goodies and baddies as to who they were and their interest in the proceedings.

As prosecution expert witness I, along with the defence expert witness, were allowed to be present in court throughout the proceedings in order to advise our respective counsel on various points if required to do so. I plonked myself down next to Ann. The lawyers took their respective positions at the front in the following order. First in line was the RSPCA's prosecution lawyer, followed by the four defence lawyers, in the middle of whom sat their expert witness, Leemax from the Dwyryd Hunt case in Blaenau Ffestiniog.

Amidst the passing of a few pleasantries, they set about plugging in their laptops and retrieving bulging A4 folders from the depths of their briefcases. At this point it became blatantly obvious that the single lawyer representing the RSPCA was well and truly outgunned by the four representing the defendants and to make matters worse one of them was the large, rotund chap in the oversized suit I had overheard on the bench outside!

I whispered to Ann, "Blimey, he was referring to me!!' Looks like I'm in for a bit of a grilling!!

Eventually the court usher gave the command, 'all rise' as the judge entered to take his seat at the bench. After a few words with counsel, he summoned the court usher to bring in the defendants.

Heads turned towards the back of the courtroom as Christian Adam Latcham, Jamie Richard Rush, Cyle Griffin Jones, and Thomas Lawrence Young entered amidst the occasional mutter of encouragement from a relative or friend as they took their seats in the dock.

Day one of the proceedings began with various lengthy dialogues to the court by counsel followed by calling the first witness in the form of the undercover journalist going under the pseudonym of John. Now this where things got a little heated in respect that the defence objected to the fact that 'John' would be giving evidence from behind a screen with only the judge and counsel able to actually see him. They argued that everyone should have the opportunity to see the witness whilst the prosecution argued that it was paramount to his future work and personal safety that he retained anonymity. Eventually the judge called a recess whilst counsel put their respective arguments forward.

In these circumstances you are all sat around in the public waiting area. The goodies sit on one side and the baddies on the other glowering at each other amidst whispered comments. I think it is fair to say that as far as the badger digging fraternity is concerned, I'm not the flavour of the month and it's not unusual for a few snide remarks to come my way or even a shoulder shove if they think no one's watching. But it's all part and parcel of the job and water off a ducks back.

Eventually after some thirty minutes or so the usher entered the court leaving all and sundry anticipating a recall and proceedings to reconvene. But no such luck! Out she came again, and even more time drifted on by. Tired of sitting around some paced up and down periodically glancing at their watches. Some, mainly the defendants, and presumably from nervous tension, made regular trips to the loo.

I occasionally have the vision of a defendant having heard the call over the speaker system that the court is reconvening, dashing out of the loo and down the corridor frantically tugging on his zip. And even more amusing still tugging away at it during proceedings requiring the judge to ask, "Excuse me Mr Latcham do you have a problem?"

"Err, yes, sir, me zips caught in me trousers and I can't get it up!"

Anyway, after what seemed an age, the court reconvened with the prosecution having won the deliberation and much to the frustration of the defence, 'John' was allowed to retain his anonymity. His cross examination went on for some time with the four defence lawyers taking it turn to fire questions at him. Occasionally the judge would put his own questions forward to clarify a point. Of course, I sat there watching and listening to all of this knowing full well that at some point in the proceedings it would be my turn to take the stand, not behind a screen, but in full view of the court. And as the prosecution expert witness it would be a no holds barred cross examination! But that wasn't going to be today. Time was rolling on and at 4.30 pm the judge closed the proceedings for the day to reconvene at 10am sharp the following morning.

Once out of the courtroom Ann and I made a quick exit and wandered back to the hotel to freshen up and enjoy a much-needed evening meal. I needed to clear my mind ready for the following day's proceedings knowing full well that at some point during the day I would be called to the stand. I needed to clear my mind and rather than pace around the room I grabbed my camera and wandered the streets of Cardiff city centre. It was a dark, drizzly evening, with the red, amber, and green of the traffic lights by the castle glistening a colourful reflection in the wet tarmac below.

Cars, buses, and taxis sped by sending a fine spray onto the pavement. The night sky may have been dark, but the place was alive with colour. Not just from the illuminated castle entrance and the glistening traffic lights coupled with the reflecting dipped beams of passing traffic, but also from the multitude of cafes and wine bars looking warm and inviting. As I wandered around trying my hand at a bit of street photography the lively upbeat sound of Salsa music drifted down the road from 'The Old Havana Bar' with its wide inviting entrance open to the street.

A 1950s American Cadillac took pride of place in the entrance amidst an array of brightly colourful exotic pictures adorning the walls. The place gave the impression of looking into a never-ending narrow room that seemed to go on for ever. It was rather like looking down a tunnel into a different world. Some people sat on tall bar stools sipping cocktails whilst others danced to the intoxicating music which, combined with the subdued lighting and décor, gave the impression of being lured into a strange intoxicating world that you may never return from. But I wasn't in Cardiff to enjoy myself. I was there to hopefully see four badger digging morons get their just deserts! And with that thought in mind I made my way back to the hotel and bed.

Once again, with so much going on in my mind sleep was fitful. If I wasn't thinking about the case I was trying to focus my eyes on the green luminous hands of my watch on the bedside table. Finally, it was 7 am and time to get up and with ablutions over and done with and caffeine levels topped up over breakfast we were ready to face the day. I once again changed from jeans and T-shirt into my formal attire of suit and tie.

Some fifteen minutes and we once again entered the portals of justice of Cardiff Crown Court and the inevitable nerves and feeling of trepidation began to well up inside me. No matter how many times I do this I always feel the same and will never feel comfortable with it. I fear that if you do you risk complacency and over confidence setting in. Not a good combination!

Once through the formalities of security we climbed the wide elegant staircase once again to the public waiting area. It was just as busy as the day before with lawyers dashing here there and everywhere but this time there was no time for people watching as the doors to court three swung open and it was once more unto the breach. We took our seats only to stand again as the judge emerged to reconvene and off, we went.

Various aspects of the case were discussed between counsel and judge, followed by the clandestine video footage taken by 'John' on shirt and coat cam being played on the courtroom's large screen. Despite having watched it a few times and investigated the actual site of the incident it was no less repugnant to watch than the first time. Even though no badger was actually seen in the footage the activity and language were disgusting. The cruelty inflicted on other species was vile and cruel to put it mildly. At 12 pm the judge called a recess for lunch to reconvene at 1 pm. We wandered off to the court cafe area for coffee and a bite to eat. We had just ordered our food and taken a seat when one by one the defence lawyers wandered in. Due to there not being a table to seat them together they spread around with the big fat one in the oversized suit plonking himself down opposite us. I couldn't help but stare as he gorged himself on a plate of eggs and bacon accompanied by a couple of rounds of thick toast. As he took a bite, crumbs fell from his mouth to roll down his half-mast tie like a rabble of ski jumpers, eventually tumbling off the end to roll down his shirt with buttons strained to their limit in an effort to contain the bulging belly. Not a pretty sight!!

Some defence lawyers, when out of the court room environment can, on occasions, let their veil slip a little to reveal a hint of humanity but not this one. I got the impression that he wasn't kidding when he said, "Don't worry, once I get him up there, he'll know about it!"

And boy, was I about to find out!!

10

The Fat Man In The Oversized Suit, A Defence Expert Sent Packing & A White Rabbit Comes Up Trumps

All too quickly, 1 pm arrived and it was time to reconvene. We had only just plonked our bums down when the court usher ordered, 'all rise' as the judge entered to take his seat.

A few moments later I heard the call "Will Mr Malcolm Ingham please take the stand!"

My stomach did its usual somersault as I left my seat to walk to the front of the court and the witness box. As I stepped into the box I gazed around the room. First to the throng of faces in the public gallery, then the defendants, and finally the row of people sat directly below me facing the bench. First in line was the RSPCA's prosecution lawyer, followed by two defence lawyers, then Leemax, the defence expert witness looking his usual self-satisfying, smug self, followed by a third defence lawyer and last but least, the big fat one in the oversized suit.

When I first take the stand, time seems to stand still and I'm in my own silent little world. Just me, a judge or a bench of magistrates and the lawyers. I have been in this situation far too many times to remember but despite that I still get as nervous as hell. My throat is as parched as a desert and my heart beats uncontrollably.

Suddenly I'm shaken out of my trance like state as the court usher hands me a card followed by the words, "Please read out loud the following oath."

I take the card and despite my throat feeling like a sand pit I try to project in a loud clear voice, "*I do solemnly, sincerely and truly declare that the evidence I shall give shall be the truth the whole truth and nothing but the truth.*"

She takes the card from me, and I take a sip of water from the plastic cup trying hard to hide the fact that my hand wants to shake uncontrollably. And then it begins!!

As the prosecution opens the case the adrenalin kicks in and my brain tells me to compose myself and concentrate on the matters at hand. Firstly, I confirm my name etc., followed by various questions relating to my evidence. Once finished the court hands over to the defence to put their questions to me. Now this is where the fun really begins!

As an expert witness I'm not there to be subjected to a grilling as a normal witness may have to endure. (*In inverted commas!*) In a nutshell, my job is to assist the court with regards to certain elements of the case and offer my opinion in a totally unbiased manner regardless of prosecution or defence. The problem, for the defence at least, is that I'm the key witness in respect that I gave my opinion on the covert footage. I examined the scene of the incident in question, gathered and collated the evidence, followed by submitting a prosecution report outlining my findings and conclusions.

Obviously, the defence are not going to take everything I say in the report as gospel and will try their upmost to contradict it, as their own expert witness will already have done when responding to my report. After all, their job is to get their clients off the hook which, as you can imagine, makes my role as a prosecution expert witness rather interesting to say the least!

Anyway, the first in line wasn't too bad and after thirty minutes or so advised the judge that he had no more questions and handed over to defence number two. I always equate the first in line to be rather like the first round of a boxing match in that it gives me the opportunity to relax a little and sort my mind out.

Number two was a small rather petite lady who, despite appearances, had a fearsome reputation and I fully expected a bit of a brow bashing. She didn't disappoint in the fact that she was persistent in her questioning and not one for letting go but, like the first, I had faced worse. At one point, we actually agreed in the respect that she complained to the judge that due to being a little hard of hearing, coupled with the court speaker system not working too well, she was having difficulty in fully hearing some of my responses. I sympathised and explained that I too was having a similar problem. This shared difficulty appeared to soften her a little particularly towards the end of her questioning and, considering her reputation, I thought that I had got off relatively lightly.

Number three was a little more volatile with him refusing to let go on various questions but, once again, it was no worse than anything I had experienced before, and he certainly hadn't gained any ground. The defence in general were obviously of the same opinion as whispered comments were passed amongst them along with hastily scribbled notes handed across to Leemax, who in turn scribbled his own in response. The defence were now on the back foot with everything resting on the shoulders of number four. The big fat one in the oversized suit!!

He slowly and very deliberately stood up clutching my report. He glanced at the judge, then at me, followed by a short pause after which he came at me like a raging bull. He fired a barrage of questions at me with my answers only serving to provoke him into more of a frenzy as he fired back the same question but from a slightly different slant in the hope that I would deviate from my original answer. Every now and again frustration would get the better of him when, amidst a spell of huffing and puffing, he would pause for a few seconds to work out another mode of attack. He was like a dog with a bone in that if he didn't get the answer he hoped for he would twist and turn the questions over and over again in his quest to wear me down in the hope that I would inadvertently deviate from an original answer.

At one point I was under so much intensive cross examination that Ann couldn't bear it any longer and left the courtroom. Unfortunately, when she came back ten minutes later, we were still crossing swords. Every now and again I would glance down at Leemax slouching there in his usual slovenly manner with arms folded and legs outstretched. At one point he was obviously under the false impression that the defence were finding chinks in my armour as he returned my gaze with one of his self-righteous smiles.

Finally, after what seemed an eternity, the judge intervened to inform the lawyer that it was now 4.30 pm with the proceedings scheduled to close for the day at 5 pm at the latest and did he have any more questions? He responded by saying that yes, he had, and could he have another ten minutes? Unfortunately for me his request was granted! And to say that he took full advantage of his extra time would be an understatement!

He tried every trick in the book, but he was running out of questions and out of sheer desperation resorted to plucking at straws one of which was, "Mr Ingham, have you ever given expert evidence for the defence?"

I replied that I had not.

"Ha, I thought not!" he retorted.

I explained that I had never been approached to do so, to which he strongly insinuated that due to being biased in my opinion I would refuse anyway. I felt like turning the question around in respect of asking him if his own expert witness had ever represented the prosecution but that would have overstepped the mark regarding protocol and as such bit my tongue.

After a brief pause, he came at me with his final question, "Mr Ingham, I assume that you have read the Protection of Badgers Act 1992?"

I replied that yes, I had.

He immediately fired back by asking me if I was familiar with a particular paragraph on page whatever. I explained that despite having read the Act I could not quote it parrot fashion, and as such would have to refresh my memory with regards to those particular references within the Act.

You would have thought that all his prayers had been answered in one as he dramatically threw his arms up in the air in glee whilst theatrically waving my report in the air and responded with, "Then you are obviously not familiar with the correct terminology of the Act?" followed by, "Let me remind you Mr Ingham, in your report you refer to the sett as being active at the time of your visit do you not?"

I replied, "Yes, that's correct."

Once again, he flung his arms in the air in an exaggerated gesture of jubilation as he reminded me that the correct terminology should be currently active, not active!!

At this point Leemax shuffled around in excitement as he uttered his pleasure at this discrepancy in terminology whilst the defendants, who obviously also assumed that I was at last done for, shuffled in their seats in glee.

I explained to the judge that the term currently active as opposed to active were purely and simply a diversification of terminology, meaning exactly the same thing, an active badger sett.

Despite the judge appearing to agree with my response the fat man in the oversized suit wasn't happy and continued to strongly disagree with my explanation. Finally, at 5 pm the judge intervened once more stating that in his view I had answered all the questions perfectly adequately and he was releasing me from the stand.

As you can imagine that didn't go down too well with my brow beating opponent. His face turned a dark shade of purple as his blood pressure rose to the extent that I thought he was about to blow a gasket!

Amidst a shower of saliva, he loudly spluttered, "But I have not finished with Mr Ingham!! I have more questions!"

Needless to say, judges are not accustomed to being back chatted by lawyers and the judge informed him in no uncertain terms that yes, he had indeed finished along with a reminder that it wasn't wise to argue with the judge and he should sit down and shut up.

The faces of the other defence lawyers along with Leemax dropped like a ton of bricks in the realisation that their last line of defence, the battleship in the oversized suit, had been defeated.

A feeling of immense self-satisfaction swept over me along with an almost irresistible urge to punch the air and emit a triumphant 'up yours!' Thankfully, I resisted the temptation as self-control prevailed! After his admonishment, the judge thanked me for my evidence and released me from the stand followed by closing the day's proceedings.

With me having finally taken the stand and presented my evidence I could at last relax a little. The pressure was off, and the following day would be the end of the trial. All the evidence had been heard leaving only the prosecution and defence to make their closing speeches prior to the judge's summing up. But that was for tomorrow! The priority now was to freshen up, have a meal, and enjoy a pint and a good night's sleep at long last!

The following day during their closing speeches, the defence gave their usual spiel, stating that the prosecution didn't have a case to answer and generally tried to undermine the prosecution expert statement. They also came out with the usual sob stories that their clients were the pillars of society with fifteen kids to support and another three on the way, plus being full time carers to a multitude of local residents. In other words, to find them guilty and send them off to jail would be a travesty of justice, with every man and his dog being much worse off. Oh, and by the way, he promises never to be cruel to animals ever again and he loves badgers!!!

After hearing the closing speeches, the judge called an hour's recess for his deliberations. Most decided to make the most of the time by taking the opportunity to grab a coffee or wander outside for a bit of fresh air.

Ann and I decided on the fresh air option and were a little surprised to see a throng of reporters and TV camera crews waiting outside hoping to catch a glimpse of the defendants. And they weren't to be disappointed! Within a few minutes Latcham, Jones, Rush and Young came prancing down the steps onto the street wearing fox masks and laughing and joking. They were so convinced that they were walking free that they decided to put on a show for the cameras.

With all the evidence so blatantly stacked against them it beggared belief that they could honestly believe they were going to be found not guilty; or at least in their tiny minds if by some blatant travesty of justice they were found guilty, they would receive nothing more than a slap on the wrist.

But they were to be disappointed!!

After half an hour we decided to make our way back to the public waiting area in readiness for the call back to court. Others were already there, some in little groups by the locked court room door. The defendants, still appearing to be in their jovial frame of mind mingled with their lawyers. Occasionally casting furtive glances our way whilst making some whispered comment. Eventually security arrived to put an end to their chit chat and the door was unlocked for everyone to take their seats once again.

We had just sat down when the cry came from the court usher for everyone to stand. The defendants, now back in the dock rose. A couple appeared to have lost a little of their bravado as they nervously fidgeted and shuffled around in their seats. But the likes of Latcham and Jones, forever wanting to give the impression of the hard man, persisted in their act of bluster when in truth they were probably on the verge of peeing their pants. The judge took his seat and as everyone else took theirs you could hear a pin drop.

Suddenly the silence was broken as the usher cried, 'Defendants please rise.' They stood with hands clasped to their front as they glanced at their supporters in the public gallery.

The judge gave a lengthy summary of the circumstances for them being charged with the offences along with the evidence offered to the court including the covert video footage of shirt and coat cam plus witness statements and the reports of both prosecution and defence expert witnesses. He finally concluded by finding all four guilty of all charges. Once again, he reiterated the cruelty and horrendous nature of their crimes stating that they left him with no alternative but to hand out custodial sentences. These were as follows -

Christian Latcham, 26 weeks custodial. *(Already had a life ban on keeping dogs.)*

Jones, 22 weeks custodial. *(Already had a life ban on keeping dogs plus previously served 18 weeks custodial for cruelty to dogs.)*

Jamie Rush, 22 weeks custodial.

Thomas Young, 20 weeks custodial, suspended for 12 months, plus subject to a curfew between 21.00 & 06.00 for 12 weeks. *(He also had an existing life ban from keeping dogs.)*

Their bravado had certainly dissipated somewhat as they were cuffed and led away to the van to escort them to jail.

As Jones was being led away someone in the public gallery shouted, "Keep your head up love."

Ironically, Rush successfully appealed against his conviction at Merthyr Tydfil Crown Court. The RSPCA opposed the appeal but, due to the possibility of compromising the anonymity of 'John' the undercover reporter, they decided to drop the opposition. Needless to say, Rush danced out of prison with a beaming smile free to continue his sadistically cruel pastimes as and when the fancy took him.

A few short months later I was to find myself once again in South Wales and ironically back at Llanddewi Velfrey examining the very same badger sett after it had been dug a second time. Once again, the RSPCA took the case *(RSPCA v Mathew Jones)* it was heard in Haverfordwest Magistrates Court presided over by a district judge with the defence expert witness being once again none other than yours truly, Leemax!! I arrived at the court quite early and as I sat in the public waiting area a couple sat themselves down opposite me.

As we passed a few pleasantries to pass the time who should enter but Leemax who, with a look of absolute horror, dashed over to the couple exclaiming, "You shouldn't be talking to him, he's on the other side!!" and quickly ushered them away. Little did I realise I had been chatting to the defendant and, of course, he didn't realise that he had been chatting to the prosecution's expert witness!

Unfortunately, a courts public waiting area doesn't differentiate between them and us and it's not unusual to find yourself idling your time away in very close proximity to the defendants. Not an ideal situation! In truth, once a witness has signed in, they should be immediately escorted to a witness waiting room well away from anyone else associated with the case other than a lawyer. Unfortunately, that's always the case with them often having no choice but to be in close proximity to the defendants whilst waiting to be shown to a private room.

Once again Leemax didn't disappoint and fully lived up to his reputation of attempting to twist the facts to the defence's advantage. On the final day, the defence counsel in their closing speech gave their usual waffle about their client's innocence and that he was a pillar of society. He attends church every Sunday morning and was only digging around a badger sett to look for worms so that his little lad could go fishing for minnows and he thought it would be nice to take his two little battle scarred and blood-stained terriers along for a walk at the same time.

Or words to that effect!! He also advised the judge that the prosecution expert witness report should be dismissed as evidence in that it brought nothing of relevance to the court.
(This sort of comment in the defence's closing speech is to be expected and as such doesn't worry me in the slightest.)

Not to disappoint, Leemax afforded me one of his sickly self-satisfying smirks as he lounged in his seat to the extent that he appeared to be in imminent danger slithering off.

After the closing speeches the judge retired to consider his verdict whereupon Leemax and defence counsel huddled together in a little group to merrily chat away amongst themselves.

Eventually the call came to 'all rise' as the judge re-emerged to deliver his verdict. After a short speech outlining the ins and outs of the case, he concluded that, in his opinion, the defence expert witness report brought absolutely nothing to the case. He continued by saying that in total contrast he found the prosecution expert report greatly assisted the court in finding the defendant guilty of all charges leaving him with no alternative but to deliver a custodial sentence. And the icing on the cake came when he also stated that due to the dubious nature of some of the stated facts in the defence expert report that no court costs should be awarded to Leemax. Once again, I felt the overwhelming urge to punch the air, but restraint prevailed. The judge dismissed the court followed by the cry of 'all rise' as he retired to chambers. Leemax was fuming and, with a face as black as thunder, grabbed his briefcase and scurried off.

I first came across him well over 20 years ago whilst on a case in Staffordshire and our paths have crossed many times since. You can guarantee that he will twist and turn the facts to such an extent that they are, to say the least, hanging tenuously to the factual by a mere thread. His report will totally contradict mine to the point of implying that I wouldn't know a badger if I fell over one or a badger sett if I stumbled into one.

He has blatantly fabricated evidence and produced photographs purported to have been taken in the same location as my own when they were obviously not. It never ceases to amaze me how, in badger digging/baiting cases at least, a defence expert witness (*or at least this particular one*) appears to be given far more latitude with regards to court protocol and the responsibility of an expert witness than the prosecution expert ever is.

If I were to do the same I would, in all probability, be very quickly pulled up by my breeches with the very real possibility of being officially discredited. Not only would it have serious consequences with regards to my acting as an expert in future cases, but I could also face perjury charges i.e. to knowingly make misleading or false statements under oath. It really begs the question; how on earth does he get away with it? But he does!

Despite all the intense cross examination I have endured in various courtrooms throughout the years, ever single one was worth it due to gaining a positive result. But the case that stands out the most, in total contrast to the others, is due to the fact that I was in and out of the witness box before you could say Jack Robinson and we lost!

It all started at 5.30pm on 24 May 2018. I received a call from PC Dave Allen of the North Wales Rural Crime Team asking if I could possibly attend an incident of badger digging at a location in Holt, Wrexham. The location consisted of a long narrow stretch of scrubby woodland close to houses, a market garden, and fields. A call came in from a member of the public that two men had been digging a badger sett in the wood and at the time were trying to fix a flat tyre on their vehicle parked on a nearby lane. The police quickly responded and apprehended the two suspects. They were in possession of terrier dogs and spades. When questioned they stated that they had been after rabbits. Whilst carrying out a search of the vehicle the officers discovered a blood-stained shirt. DNA tests later showed that the blood was from a badger. By the time I arrived on the scene the defendants, due to being compliant, had been allowed to leave the scene after being advised that they may face charges relating to badger offences. I carried out my usual investigation leading to a conclusion that they had in fact been digging a currently active badger sett and submitted a report. The RSPCA decided to take the case and employed a barrister (*one they hadn't used before*) to take the prosecution.

On 20th June I received a letter advising me that the case was going to be heard at Wrexham Magistrates Court on 27th June and that my attendance would be required. The case was presided over by a bench of magistrates with the defendants defended by two lawyers along with evidence from a vet. The prosecution consisted of the barrister, a vet to give evidence on his examination of the dogs, PC Dave Allen plus myself as expert witness.

Prior to the proceedings the prosecution barrister took both me and the vet to a room where he separately gave us a briefing. All I can say regarding that was that mine was very brief with him basically saying that he would keep his opening questions very short, and could I keep my responses equally short? I found his attitude to the case very strange and couldn't help but wonder what he was playing at.

I wasn't allowed in court until called to give evidence whereupon he stuck to his word in keeping his questions extremely brief. When I attempted to answer a question in detail, he would immediately stop me. After what seemed like only a few minutes he advised the bench that he had no more questions and handed over to the defence who, in turn, also advised that they had no questions. I was subsequently released to take my seat in the courtroom to listen to the rest of the proceedings.

The defendants took the stand to give evidence which, if nothing else, proved to be slightly entertaining in that they were both as thick as two short planks and struggled to put two words together. When one of them was asked about the blood on the shirt his excuse was that his dog had run from the wood into the field and been kicked by a cow. In his bid to retrieve the dog, he had to give chase and rugby tackle it. The story became even more ridiculous when he followed on by saying that an injured badger must have bled in the field leaving a pool of blood which the dog must have ran through and stained his shirt when he rugby tackled it!! Believe that and you believe that the moons made of green cheese!!

At one point he was handed a map of the area in question and asked to point out where the dog was kicked in relation to the badger sett. After a few minutes of staring at it in total bewilderment his lawyer who, with a wry smile, had to advise him that he was actually holding the map upside down.

Finally, after turning it this way and that, he pointed a grubby finger at a spot on the map stating, "I fink it was there!!"

He also addressed the chair of the bench as love, and his lawyer as mate! Neither bothered to correct him on how to address either the bench or a lawyer. Ironically, the bench found them not guilty!! As I left the court to walk to the car park the pair were in front of me laughing and joking as they literally danced their way to their car.

Dave and I still talk about the case and remain in total bewilderment as to how they got away with it, plus what on earth was the prosecution barrister playing at?!! Had he done a deal with the defence? We will never know but one thing's for sure, the RSPCA won't be using him again.

One possible explanation could be that the defence, if they consider the prosecution expert report strong and compelling, will on occasions try to persuade the court that it's not relevant and therefore inadmissible. Whilst on the other hand if they consider it a weak report it's to their advantage to have it presented by the prosecution. But I guess we will never know one way or the other?

In total contrast to the above was the case of the White Rabbit. Nothing to do with Nivens McTwisp, the white rabbit in Tim Burton's film adaptation of Lewis Carroll's *Alice in Wonderland*, but definitely a classic example of the ups and downs and twists and turns of wildlife crime prosecutions.

It was a Thursday, 25th August 2022. I was in the conservatory enjoying my morning coffee whilst watching a busy flock of long-tailed tits flitting to and fro from my fat ball bird feeder to the elder bush by the kitchen window when my mobile rang. As I picked it up to take the call the screen read 'number withheld' meaning that in all probability it was a call from the North Wales Police Rural Crime Team and a job. As it turned out it wasn't a job as such but an officer requiring advice. He started by asking if I knew of anyone who could give a statement stating that there were no wild white rabbits in the UK. I explained that no one with hand on heart could give such a statement whereupon he gave a deep sigh and remarked that he didn't expect the case to go anywhere anyway and thanked me for my time.

Before he could hang up I asked him why he needed it and he explained that on 21st December 2021, a guy had put a video of himself on a particular social media site stood in a field and placing a white rabbit on the ground whereupon it was encouraged to run, at which point he released a running dog (*lurcher type*) to chase, catch and retrieve it. Then he broke its neck! The video was seen by a member of the public who reported it to the police resulting in them tracking him down. Some days later the police and the RSPCA carried out a warrant raid at his address which proved futile in respect that nothing of any consequence was found. Many months had passed since then with the general consensus of opinion being that they were clutching at straws with regards to a prosecution, hence the call from the officer. The reason he needed such a tenuous statement that there were no wild white rabbits in the UK was due to the fact that wild rabbits are not a protected species and can be legally hunted with up to two dogs with the landowner's permission. Now we come to the crunch of the matter as to why he was looking for such a statement!

Under the Animal Welfare Act of 2006, it is an offence to cause unnecessary suffering to a domestic animal. In 2021, Parliament passed an amendment to the Act, increasing the maximum custodial sentence from six months to five years allowing it to be heard in either magistrate or crown court. Obviously, the guy was claiming that despite being white the rabbit was in fact wild and not a domestic pet rabbit and he had the landowner's permission to be there. He also claimed that he had caught the rabbit in order to train his young dog to chase, catch and retrieve rabbits.

After listening to his reason, I explained that despite not being able to give him the statement he was hoping for I was prepared to give him a statement explaining the likelihood on a scale of one to ten of the rabbit actually being a white wild rabbit along with the reasons for my score. Inevitably from time-to-time domestic rabbits either escape or are abandoned out in the countryside and end up living feral and interbreeding with the truly wild population. The problem is that they are not acclimatised to the unpredictability of our weather, particularly during the winter months and don't survive very long. Any hybrid offspring produced can usually be identified by their mixed colour variation and more often than not their head shape; domesticated rabbits tend to have a stubbier head and snout than truly wild ones.

Anyway, I submitted a report stating the ins and outs of the likelihood of the rabbit in question being wild born along with stating that, as the Flintshire Vice County Mammal Record verifier for many years I had never had a record of a wild white rabbit submitted to me for verification. To be honest I really didn't expect the case to go to court but how wrong can you be. A few weeks later notification from the Criminal Justice System popped through my letter box explaining that on 9th November 2022, my presence was requested at Caernarfon Magistrates Court to give expert evidence on behalf of the prosecution in the case against Daniel Robert Gilmore.

The following day the officer rang to say, "Sorry Malcolm, I really didn't think this was going anywhere!"

On the day of the hearing my wife Ann and I were sat in the witness waiting room (*Caernarfon Court is the exception to the rule in that they actually follow procedure and allow you the privacy of a witness waiting room upon arrival*) when the door opened and a young lawyer clutching a bundle of papers came striding through to introduce herself. She sat herself down and whilst proceeded to run through the case raised a question which led her to enquire whether or not I had actually seen the video. She was a little surprised when I explained that I hadn't and that my report was simply based off a verbal description from the officer. She explained that it was vital that I view the footage before deciding to proceed and quickly escorted me to another room to view the said footage on her laptop.

She explained that my conclusions after viewing the footage would be the deciding factor on whether or not we went into court. After watching it a number of times I concluded that, as stated in my report, the man was indeed releasing a domestic rabbit to be chased by a dog. The call to court came a few minutes later presided over by a bench of magistrates along with defence and prosecution lawyers plus the defendant and yours truly as the sole witness.

The defence lawyer was accustomed to defending badger diggers and baiters (*Ironically, he was the defence lawyer who lost the latest case of David Thomas of the Dwyryd Hunt in Blaenau Ffestiniog under the Animal Welfare Act. Sentence reduced on appeal!*) and as such, very familiar with the twists and turns of defending this type of case. He had obviously done his homework and came armed with a few questions that he hoped would open up a discrepancy or two in my report to put me on the back foot. But unlike many of his colleagues that I've crossed swords with, he wasn't unduly bombastic or aggressive in his approach. His questions were methodical, with my responses generating a brief pause, whereupon he would reposition his specs and take a downward glance at his notes in preparation for his next question. Or as is often the case in these circumstances the same question but worded slightly differently in the hope that you deviate from your original answer.

He kept me in the witness stand for quite some time with questions and answers going back and forth with me on a number of occasions explaining to the bench why I disagreed with a certain aspect of a question whilst adding more clarification.

Eventually he responded with, "No more questions your worships," and I was stood down.

The defendant was next to be called to the stand where, whilst under questioning by the prosecution, he stubbornly stated that the location of the incident was literally overflowing with white wild rabbits, and he couldn't understand what all the fuss was about. At one stage he began to lose it a little and whilst looking directly at me stated that he was an experienced hunter of rabbits and strongly disagreed with my opinions regarding the rabbit in question. Eventually the magistrates retired for their verdict, and I must admit that despite putting forward a strong case I wasn't too optimistic with regards to a positive outcome.

But how wrong can you be? They returned a short while later whereupon the chair of the bench gave a brief summing up of the case before returning a guilty verdict of causing 'unnecessary suffering to a domestic animal' under the Welfare Animal Act. He was summoned to return to court a few weeks later for sentencing, ultimately receiving a 12-week custodial suspended for 12 months, plus court costs and fines to a total of £868.

To compare this with the Wrexham badger digging case really highlights the fact that the final outcome can never be taken for granted. No matter how strong and well-presented your prosecution report may be or how well you have unbendingly stood by your evidence under cross examination, you can never predict the result. I mentioned previously that I place far more faith in a district judge than a bench of magistrates. But they certainly came up trumps on this case.

I have lost count of the number of times I have given expert evidence over the years, with over 90% ending in a guilty verdict. As mentioned before you can never guarantee a positive outcome, but the odds are definitely more favourable if a strong case is presented to the court coupled with an experienced expert witness. Due to the fact that expert witnesses within the field of wildlife crime are thin on the ground the National Wildlife Crime Unit, in September 2023, funded an 'Expert Witness Training' course organised by the Badger Trust, to be held at the NAEC Stoneleigh Park, Warwickshire.

The focal point of the course was to offer training to individuals who may be considering the prospect of becoming a CPS (Crime Prosecution Service) recognised expert witness within their individual wildlife/conservation field of expertise. The curriculum covered the role of an expert witness, court procedure, writing reports, and giving evidence, as well as the individual duties of both prosecution and defence experts and their eventual mutual engagements in order to find a middle ground within their respective reports.

I first heard about the course during a conversation with PC Dave Allen of the North Wales Police Rural Crimes Team who happened to mention that he had been speaking to Craig Fellowes, the Badger Trust's Wildlife Crime and Training Officer. I was interested in respect that, as far as I was aware, this was a first and out of interest contacted Craig. He explained that the course was aimed mainly at prospective expert witnesses within the realms of wildlife crime. He also went on to say that due to my many years of doing the job, coupled with the glowing references he had heard from the police and RSPCA, I was already a recognised expert, but it would be great to have me there if I thought it worthwhile.

The course itself was free with the only cost being travel and accommodation and more out of curiosity than anything else I decided to attend. I booked at the Stoneleigh Park Hotel which was literally a five-minute walk away from the course venue and drove down on the Sunday ready for the course on Monday. I was up bright and early the following morning to give myself plenty of time for a shower and a leisurely breakfast before making my way to the venue for a 10 am start.

The course was run by a Training Consultancy firm specialising in training police and others in becoming an expert witness. The tutor was an ex-drugs squad police officer who, on his own admission, was clueless about anything associated with wildlife. A total of fourteen people from around the UK attended consisting of ten in person and four via zoom. Out of the fourteen, nine had no court experience whatsoever but due to their role within a wildlife/conservation environment, felt that it was only a matter of time before they could be called to give evidence and considered it wise if it was presented by a recognised expert. Out of the ten in the room, five were already experienced investigators and expert witnesses.

These included: one RSPCA Inspector specialising in wildlife crime and law: three National Wildlife Crime Unit Investigators, two of which worked on raptor persecution whilst the third investigated crimes under CITES (*The Convention on*

International Trade in Endangered Species) and myself as an investigator and expert witness in badger related offences.

To be perfectly honest I found the course lacking in actuality. It was simply a classroom exercise consisting of a multitude of sections taken from the CPS guidelines. Certain elements such as the role of an expert witness and court procedure and protocol etc. were obviously relevant but others were textbook exercises that didn't go hand in hand with the reality of being an expert witness within the field of wildlife crime. I was the first to raise a couple of points which was soon followed by others experienced in the reality of the twists and turns of giving expert evidence. Some of my comments were 'hang on a minute, that's not quite how it works in the real world' and I particularly questioned the subject with regards to the prosecution and defence experts getting their heads together in order to find common ground followed by submitting a 'Joint Statement of Expert Witnesses'.

To emphasise the point, I mentioned the underhand methods of Leemax to manipulate the truth to the defence's advantage to which the tutor responded, "But he can't do that!'

My response was, "But he does and what's more, he gets away with it!"

I also brought up the fact that in all my years of acting as a prosecution expert witness, only once had the court requested that I contact the defence expert with a view to compiling a joint statement. Once again, the expert in question was none other than Leemax and needless to say I thought it a pointless exercise. But the court had requested it and as such I rang him to explain that a joint statement had been requested, his response was as I expected and totally negative stating that he didn't see the point. At least we finally agreed on something!!

Anyway, the conversation ended with him saying, "Fine, if the court wants it, you write it and say what you want." End of conversation! I submitted the joint statement with the first paragraph summarising my conversation with Leemax and his opinion on the subject of a joint statement.

Anyway, back to the course. I, along with others, had issues with other topics such as the process of cross examination, which to my mind he put across as being a rather polite and civilised affair.

Pity no one had told the fat man in the oversized suit!!

Despite the course being quite full on, I couldn't help but come to the conclusion that it didn't fully achieve its purpose in preparing prospective expert witnesses for the reality. I certainly got the impression from those initially considering the role that after listening to the comments from those of us already doing it, they hadn't fully appreciated the reality.

At the end of the course the Badger Trust Wildlife Crime and Training Officer who, as well as organising it, was actually a participant, asked all who attended to provide feedback. The hope was that if the course was deemed successful, the National Wildlife Crime Unit may consider funding another. Considering that he asked for truthful feedback I agreed that courses of this nature are needed but ideally need to be run by a police officer experienced in investigating wildlife crime in conjunction with an experienced expert witness. The two work side by side in the field with the expert gathering and collating evidence, submitting a report, and finally giving expert evidence. They could tell it as it really is, no frills, just straight down the line in order to give future potential experts a true picture of what it actually entails.

One very important element of any case that was completely absent from the course, and the very first building block of any successful prosecution, was investigating an incident along with gathering, collating and presenting solid evidence in an easily understood report. The defence have endeavoured to discredit me on more than one occasion, and will no doubt continue to do so, but they fail due to my evidence and reports telling the facts as found and without bias; and more often than not that's what comes to the fore and gains prosecutions.

Being an expert witness is time consuming and at times stressful. People will often pose the question, why do you do it?

In truth, only a masochist would admit to enjoying it! You do it because it gives you the opportunity to at least try and get some justice for our relentlessly persecuted wildlife. Whether it be badger digging and baiting, illegal fox hunting, hare coursing, deer poaching, raptor persecution or the stealing of wild bird eggs or whatever, wildlife needs people on their side.

11

The Nutter Clan Badgers & Fox Meet An Otter & On Telly Again!

Well, what can I tell you about the Nutter clan? My predicament here is the fact that there is so much to tell it's knowing where to start! I suppose I should begin with their handle, 'The Nutter Clan,' and the reason for it. The simple answer to that question is the fact they are constantly getting up to mischief in a comical sort of way and forever charging around like a bunch of demented imps in their games of catch me if you can.

They live in a large, old, well-established sett on a slope leading down to pasture and a centuries old pond and a small meandering river beyond. The sett is situated on very private land owned by a sympathetic farmer and his wife who for many years have enjoyed the clans nightly visits up to the 17th century farmhouse for their peanut treats scattered below the large study window overlooking the old tree lined drive. They even scatter a few on the low stone study window ledge where the badgers scramble up to be merely the thickness of a pane of ancient glass away from their observers.

I've monitored and recorded the Nutter clan for many years now and captured some wonderful trail camera video footage of their lives throughout the seasons. From a badger sow in late February or early March moving her tiny squealing cubs from one section of the sett to another, to around mid to late April when they make their first venture above ground to totter around on wobbly little legs (*Badgers can give birth from mid to late December through to mid-June but this is exceptional with the peak periods being from mid-January to mid-February*)

At this early stage of their lives, they are far too young to wander far from the immediate vicinity of the sett and stick close to mum's side emitting loud whickering cries of distress if they temporarily lose sight or scent of her. But they needn't worry, she's amazingly attentive and protective and soon back by their side fussing over them.

As April flows into May the cubs are coming on in leaps and bounds, gaining in strength and confidence and overflowing with an overabundance of energy that is spent on continuous non-stop play in games of catch-me-if-you-can and constant rough and tumbles which is obviously infectious as even adults often join in the games. *(The survival of cubs is very much dependant on a number of factors but particularly the weather. A dry spring followed by an equally dry, hot summer can turn the earth into a hard barren desert, making foraging for worms, grubs and other food very difficult often resulting in cub fatalities, either through the sows milk drying up or, if weaned, unable to find adequate food)*

Despite their rapid development, they are still too young to follow mum or other clan members on their nightly foraging expeditions. But, after the energy sapping process of giving birth combined with the many weeks of suckling, weaning, and nurturing she needs to begin to spend more time away foraging to build her strength back up and replace lost weight

Badgers are very family orientated animals with a strong hierarchy and tightly knit social bonds within the clan. It's exactly this that allows the sow, despite her cubs being too young to leave unsupervised, to eventually spend time venturing farther afield to forage for food in the knowledge that her cubs will be watched over by another clan member who, may or may not be related, will be designated the task of ensuring that the cubs don't wander off and that they remain safe until mum returns - in other words, a babysitter!

A couple of years ago I captured some amazing footage of the big alpha boar who having drawn the short straw regarding babysitting duties, lay flat on his back with legs akimbo where, amidst a cacophony of excited whickering, half a dozen boisterous cubs clambered all over him. Two or three would use his ample tummy as a trampoline, whilst others savaged his tail like terriers squabbling over a rat. To say he had the patience of a saint would be an understatement!

In fact, going by the expression of delight on his face he genuinely appeared to be relishing all the attention. (*Baby sitting by other clan members is known as* Alloparenting *and normally carried out by a none breeding sow*)

Around mid to the end of May the sow will begin the gradual process of introducing them to solid food and weaning them off milk. She will forage for worms and grubs around the area of the sett which she will show to the cubs and encourage them to do the same.

Some years ago I read a book, the title of which has faded from my memory, which stated that badgers did not take food into the sett but, contrary to this, one early June evening I captured trail camera footage of a sow returning to the sett with a freshly killed rabbit which she deliberately waved around in front of her cubs. Obviously, this grabbed their attention to the point where they began to squabble over it. At this point she teased them even more until one or the other tried to take it from her. Eventually she took it deep into the sett with the cubs still pulling and tugging at it. Basically, she was saying this is food and I'm in no doubt that they would have continued to pull and tug at it until it began to tear it apart whereupon it would have been devoured.

Again, I captured similar footage one July evening of three cubs emerging from the sett squabbling over the remains of a young rabbit.

In 2023 only one cub was born within the clan. This isn't unusual as generally speaking only sows holding a certain status within a clan will give birth to between one and four cubs, with two to three being the most common. A number of factors can influence the birth rate such as disturbance, weather, and food availability etc. A full and comprehensive chapter could be taken up with such topics as mating, delayed implantation, and the various reasons for implantation failure etc., but this isn't a book on the reproductive ins and outs of *Meles meles* but of my observations within a particular family group.

Anyone wishing to delve further into such topics are recommended to read what I regard to be, for me at least, the holy grail of badger books, *The Natural History Of Badgers* by Ernest Neal, published in 1986. His first book, *The Badger*, a monograph published in 1948 by Collins in the New Naturalist Series was followed his second book, *Badgers*, published in 1977 by Blandford press in the Blandford Mammal Series. This was a greatly updated version of the first book and then of course, his third book published in 1986. I corresponded with him in the mid 1980's and highly value the signed copy of *The Badger* which he very kindly sent to me. It sits on my bookshelf upon my ever-expanding collection of natural history and badger books, some dating back to the early 1800's. They make interesting if not rather outlandish reading!

The Sportsman's Directory of 1823 briefly touches on the species under the heading 'Hunting the Badger' where he states, to quote- *He lies in very strong earth, full of chambers, in zig zag directions, in the day-time. At night he goes out in pursuit of his prey; at the same time go and bag all the holes at earth; place some men to watch them; then go and draw with some sticking dogs of the bull-terrier kind. Perhaps he may be a mile from home; therefore you must make casts round, and if you know of pasture grounds where cows feed, or have fed, most likely you will find him there, turning over the dung to get to the grubs, or he may be after game, When you see cow-dung turned over, and moss collected into large heaps in cover, be assured it is a badger; his faints will likewise lie about where he frequents. On being disturbed he immediately runs home, where the bags will receive him, make a fire upon his earths, which will keep him out. The male is called a boar and the young ones pigs.*

Another in my collection published in 1898 some 72 years later titled *The Badger* by Alfred E Pease goes into far more detail with regards to the badger in general plus such topics as digging and equipment. These books really emphasize how little was actually known about the species in those days and some of the ridiculous myths that was attached to them

The Life and Habits of The Badger by J. Fairfax published in 1914 covers many aspects of the badger assumed correct at the time. Topics include the badgers habits etc. plus sport (*badger digging/baiting*) to folklore, here he mentions that in ancient times it was thought that the badger was related to the bear, with two species living in England i.e. the badger that we know today and the pig badger, with cloven hooves.

But he does state that, to quote-

Few animals has there been more nonsense written about in regards to habits and anatomy with no foundations whatsoever for the many myths relating to old Brock."

Sadly, that quote, is as relevant now as it was way back then in 1914!

Since the publication of Ernest Neal's 1986 book, more recent badger books are out there containing more up to date field observations and scientific information such as *Badger* by Timothy Roper, published in 2010 in the Collins New Natural History Library. I'm often asked if I could recommend a no nonsense, easy to read quick fact guide to badgers and I always recommend Michael Clark's excellent little book, *Badgers* published by Whittet Books. But despite the passing of time, *The Natural History of Badgers* by Ernest Neal is still my favourite go to book.

Anyway, I've digressed far too long with my nattering about books so, let's return to the Nutter clan's lone 2023 cub; and what a mad, attention seeking little rascal it was too!! Obviously with no siblings to play with, mum got its utter and complete undivided attention whether she wanted it or not. And like the babysitting boar, she had the patience of a saint. On one particular occasion she was stood by the sett looking out over the field towards the river. Something had obviously got her undivided attention other than her offspring which, as far as the cub was concerned, just wasn't on. It tried it's very best to get her attention but quickly realised that bouncing around her and no amount of whickering wasn't getting the desired effect, so it decided on a more forceful approach by grabbing hold of her tail and constantly and vigorously shaking and tugging at it for all its worth.

It may as well have been screaming, 'Mum, you're ignoring me, I want to play!' But its efforts went totally unheeded as she continued to nonchalantly gaze out over the field. At one point she turned to give it a half-hearted rebuke but no sooner had she taken up her post again it was back with a vengeance to once more take its frustration out on mum's tail.

As the weeks and months passed its attention seeking ways certainly didn't lesson with age. If anything, they increased to the extent that it became the clan's number one plaything. It became pretty obvious that as far as the rest of the clan were concerned that, if bored, let's go and rag junior. To be fair he brought most of it upon himself by the fact that he was usually the main instigator but when it got a bit too rough for his liking, and finding himself totally outnumbered, he would let out a few piercing whickerings in the hope that mum would come to the rescue. Occasionally she would intervene but more often than not she was obviously of the opinion that he was coming to no harm, plus the fact that it would toughen him up and teach him a few lessons in self-defence. She was of course proven right time and time again in that no matter how much of a playful battering he got he just bounced back for more. It was pretty obvious that junior was going all out to gain his black belt in the badger version of martial arts.

One of his favourite tricks was to charge around goading the others into a rough and tumble where, once he had the ball rolling, he would dive headfirst down a vertical hole to escape the melee. Once in the security of his bolt hole he would spend the next ten minutes or so popping up and down like a Jack-in-the-Box. It was so amusing to watch as all you could see was a badger's head and a face full of devilment, there one minute and gone the next, repeated over and over again. Every once in a while, if he thought they were tiring of the game he would jump out to wind them all up again, only to dive back into his vertical shaft to repeat his Jack-in-the-Box trick. And they say animals don't have a sense of play and that it's merely instinctive behaviour to sort out the leaders from the followers.

What a load of cobblers!!!

Yes, rough and tumbles are all part and parcel of their education and do play an important part in determining hierarchies within the clan but badgers are intelligent creatures with a strong family bond who relish family life, whether it be mutual grooming, cleaning out the sett chambers of old bedding to renew with fresh or just downright play.

By July, the cubs are now following mum and other clan members on their nightly foraging expeditions and, to a great extent, this where their education really begins. They become familiar with the clan's home range, the safest crossing sections of the river, the old fallen trees that form natural bridges, where to find the best foraging areas and hopefully, how to avoid danger. They will encounter badgers from neighbouring clans, some related, some not. Hopefully prior to these encounters they will have mastered the pros and cons of badger etiquette which should stand them in good stead when meeting individuals from a neighbouring clan. They will of course also come into contact with other species such as fox and otter and obviously due to the Nutter clan's sett being so close to the river, the badger and the otter will often cross the same paths. And take it from me, the otter is definitely the boss!

Every night the Nutter clan, once emerged from their slumbers deep within the set, will hang around in a social group for a while before wandering off. Some partake in mutual grooming and strengthening clan bonds, whilst others sit on their backsides relishing in the delights of a good old scratch. First tummies, then legs, back of heads, indeed anywhere they can reach. This ritual can go on for ages as they savour the delights of each other's company until eventually they gradually slip off into the night to forage the woods and fields, sometimes as a group, sometimes individually.

They descend down the bank towards the pond following the distinctive track, flattened and worn by generations of their kind as they head towards the river and the big ancient fallen oak branch that forms a natural bridge from the sett to the fields beyond. Just about everything uses this spot from badger, fox, rabbit, squirrel, rat, stoat and weasel to cross from one side to the other, as well as the otter who will often climb out of the water onto the natural bridge to rest for a while before slipping once more into the river. I've also recorded a plethora of bird species here from the run of the mill garden birds, to heron, little egret, mallard and mandarin ducks to kingfisher, dipper, sparrow hawk and buzzard to name but a few. For many years now this spot has provided me with some magical wildlife trail cam footage but the most memorable was on 6th Nov 2021 at 9.25pm.

One of the Nutter clan was heading for home and had just scrambled onto the bridge when the dog otter appeared heading downstream. As one spotted the other, the otter paused to stare at the badger, who in turn paused to stare at the otter. Suddenly the otter dived below the surface to vanish from sight. The badger, now totally perplexed as to where the otter had vanished to, stepped farther onto the bridge and as he approached the middle he paused for a moment or two to scan both up and downstream in his quest to discover where his aquatic cousin might be. (*Badgers and otters are both of the Mustelidae family as are stoats, weasels, polecats and pine martins*) Eventually, having seen no sign of the otter he decided to retrace his steps and turned to slowly make his way from whence he came. He had only gone a short way before he paused once again. He looked down towards the water but could see no sign of the otter. Once again, he gazed upstream but as he did so he was totally unaware that the otter had surfaced downstream and was now directly behind him with its head just above the water and eyes fixed firmly on him.

Suddenly it lunged out of the water like a great white shark to give the badger an almighty head butt on the backside after which, amidst an almighty splash, turned to vanish once more into the depths. The poor badger almost leapt off the bridge in total shock at this sudden attack to his rear but thankfully instead of joining the otter in the river he made a mad dash to the bank where he quickly spun around to face his tormentor, who of course was now nowhere to be seen. The badger, having received nothing more than a dent to his pride shook himself, presumably in an effort to compose himself and retrieve what little was left of his dignity before continuing, albeit rather cautiously, his traverse across the bridge and home.

Another otter / badger encounter captured on one of my trail cameras involved not a member of the Nutter clan but a badger from of an unnamed clan that regularly crosses the river some distance upstream and due to the absence of any form of bridge, natural or otherwise, had no choice but to paddle or on some occasions swim across to the far bank. On this particular night the river was in a gentle mood as it sedately flowed over gravel and rocks on its meandering journey downstream. The badger came trundling along as usual to eventually arrive at the water's edge where he paused for a moment or two to snuffle around amongst the pebbles and bankside vegetation. Eventually, after sucking up the odd worm or two he, waded in.

The river was so low that the water only just about reached his belly but this time instead of paddling across to the far bank upon reaching the middle he turned to head upstream totally oblivious to the fact that a large dog otter was heading downstream towards him. Old Brock was obviously in no great hurry occasionally pausing where, with water gently lapping at his belly, he would gaze around and sniff the night air.

As already mentioned, the river was very low and as such the otter, like the badger, was paddling his way up when he suddenly spotted the badger heading directly towards him. He stopped dead in its tracks and lay low and motionless with the water gently flowing around him. His dark wet coat blended his sleek body so well into his surroundings that he was almost invisible. He was only visible on my trail camera due to the infra-red night vision LED's picking up his bright twinkling eyes hovering just above the water.

The badger, still completely unaware of the otter's presence, continued nonchalantly on his way until he literally bumped smack bang into the otter! The pair reared up on their hind legs and amidst a cacophony of squeals and grunts, they pawed away at each other sending sprays of water flying off in all directions. It was all over in a matter of seconds as the badger, who had obviously decided that to turn tail and flee was preferable to battling it out with a large dog otter, and amidst a clamour of splashing water he made a frantic dash for the bank.

Thankfully neither were any worse off for the encounter and after observing the badger's backside disappearing up the far bank and off into the trees the otter sedately continued his journey as if the event had never taken place.

I capture trail camera footage of badger/otter interaction fairly regularly, but in September 2023, I recorded my first otter and fox interaction, which is quite surprising considering that all three use the same routes by the river on a nightly basis. The dog otter had just climbed out of the water and settled himself down in the wide-open ended section of the hollow trunk of an ancient and slowly disintegrating fallen tree traversing the river. He had just made himself comfortable when a young fox came sauntering along and I can only assume by its obvious curiosity that this was its first encounter with an otter.

It strode around the front of the fallen tree a few times in typical fox fashion when not quite sure about something. It went left then right, cautiously creeping a little closer before backing off again, only to repeat the process whilst never taking its eyes off the otter. This went on for some time with the otter trying to ignore the fact that a curious young whipper snapper of a fox was being a pest and interrupting his afternoon nap. At one point the fox actually scampered up onto the tree to peer down at the otter before eventually jumping off to resume its pacing back and forth.

Curiosity was now really getting the better it as it slowly but surely approached closer and closer to the hollow and the by now rather fed-up otter. And then the inevitable happened! The fox crept too close for comfort and the otter decided enough was enough. Amidst a cacophony of angry grunts, the otter leapt out of the hollow to chase the fox away after which he returned to continue his afternoon siesta. The fox, now having satisfied his curiosity, returned to saunter by a few minutes later this time giving the hollow tree a wide birth. Another lesson learnt for a young inquisitive fox! Don't mess with an otter!!

Badgers are intelligent, single-minded individuals who, once they have set their mind on something, will move heaven and earth to achieve their goal. I've already touched upon the fact that badgers are very partial to the occasional peanut treat with the Nutter clan being no exception. Every evening just after dusk they follow the age-old tradition of wandering up to the old farmhouse above the sett in the knowledge that a few peanut treats await them. Every evening, a dish would be filled with peanuts ready to be scattered from the old, galvanised dustbin, the sort we used to have prior to the advent of wheelie bins. For many years, the bin had been kept in an open doored storeroom adjacent to the yard without an issue; that is until one of the wily Nutter clan stumbled upon the fact that that was where the peanuts were kept.

Well, that was it! From that moment on, old Brock went on a nightly peanut bin raiding foray. In the morning, the bin lid would be on the floor, with the shredded remnants of the brown paper sack the peanuts came in scattered around the stone flagged floor. I decided to set up a trail camera to record the culprit in action. And not to disappoint, the robber arrived in the early hours to saunter up to the bin and whilst standing on his hind legs, with a flick of his snout sent the lid flying off to make one hell of racket as it spun around on the hard floor. Now you would have expected the din alone to have sent him scurrying off in a panic, but not this fella! He completely ignored the sound of metal loudly clunking around on stone to clamber headfirst into the bin to gorge himself on peanuts.

Obviously, this state of affairs couldn't go on and it was decided that the best course of action would be to lash the lid firmly down with rope in the hope that this would deter him. The following night the raider arrived on cue, ambled up to the bin and attempted to nudge the lid off in his usual way. At first, he was a little perplexed as to why it wouldn't budge, and then sheer frustration and a badger's dogged determination took over. He began to frantically paw at the rope it until he had loosened or stretched it just enough for him to create a bigger gap for him get his snout in a little further whereupon he would once again attempt to flip it off only for it to come crashing back down again.

After numerous failed attempts, sheer exasperation completely took over, as he frantically ran around the bin in an attempt to find another way in and when that failed, he began to bite at the rope. On more than one occasion he turned towards the door as if finally admitting defeat only to turn and pause for a few seconds before trying again. This went on for a few nights until it was decided to move the bin and its contents to a more secure and badger proof location.

I've utilised trail cameras to record the daily lives of the Nutter clan along with the Dickens and No-Tail clan for many years now and despite having been involved with badgers for over thirty-five years, can still be surprised at some of the events captured on camera. For some years now I have had a large fiberglass circular bath in the wood by the house which was originally manufactured and sold as an extra-large bird bath aimed at falconers housing large birds of prey such as eagles etc. I acquired a couple many years ago when I was involved in caring for and rehabilitating sick or injured birds of prey at my Wildlife Rehabilitation Unit during my ranger / wildlife officer days.

Thankfully when I retired, I had the foresight to hang on to them and now they now provide a valuable source of fresh water for a wide variety of species. On this particular occasion on 25 May 2022, the weather had been unseasonably hot and dry for well over a week when at 8pm one of the No-Tail clan came trotting through the wood at a fair old pace and literally dived into the bath. He was panting heavily and clearly uncomfortably hot and obviously relishing the relative coolness of the water. He lay on his side and on his back splashing water all over himself for a good ten minutes. Eventually after sufficiently cooling off he finally climbed out to vigorously shake himself sending sprays of water flying here there and everywhere before trotting off to vanish deep into the wood. A few days later the camera captured footage a stoat taking respite from the heat by doing exactly the same. The diversity of species taking advantage of this permanent supply of clean water never ceases to amaze me, not only during hot, dry spells but year-round. It's a regular thirst-quenching spot for badger, fox, rabbit and even the diminutive wood mouse.

A plethora of bird species also take advantage of it for bathing and drinking, with everything from blue tit to wintering redwing to tawny owl, buzzard, and sparrow hawk to name but a fraction. One of the most exciting was in February 2023 when I recorded an immature female goshawk drinking and bathing from the bath before hopping onto the trunk of a fallen tree to shake the water from its feathers and preen. It was totally relaxed and remained on the fallen tree just gazing around with one leg tucked under its belly. Eventually it turned to silently vanish deeper into the wood, zig zagging between the trees as it went. A few days later whilst following the various trails in the wood I stumbled across a large untidy looking nest at the very top of a tall spindly Scots pine tree. A large fern a few metres from its base was splattered in white bird poo confirmed that the nest was in use and to add confirmation to the species, an adult male goshawk landed in an adjacent tree.

This was the first conclusive evidence that goshawks were indeed breeding in the wood and, needless to say, from that moment on I stayed well clear and left them in peace in the knowledge that if I wished to monitor the nest I would have to apply for, and be granted, a licence. Due to the fact that the chicks had already fledged I decided that a licence would be more beneficial the following season. I actually captured more footage of a second juvenile perched on a large moss-covered boulder regularly used as a sparrow hawk plucking stone.

A great deal of my trail camera footage is shared on social media, often generating a request from various groups and organisations for permission to use it. Sometimes they may be putting an educational presentation together to show to schools, or as is more often the case, a presentation to hopefully dispel some of the myths regarding badgers predating on sheep or lambs which of course they do not! Over the years I've amassed hours upon hours of badger, sheep and lamb interaction with never the slightest hint that badgers are a danger to sheep or their lambs.

In fact, it is just the opposite and particularly so with the Nutter clan who have always shared their space with sheep who for whatever reason have a preference to spending their nights lounging around by the set. It's quite surreal to watch badgers just going about their business whether it be gathering bedding, mutual grooming or charging around like a bunch of lunatics in a game of tag, whilst a flock of sheep just lounge around contentedly chewing their cud. I've recorded footage of a gang of boisterous lambs chasing an adult badger back into the set.

A ewe with her tiny lambs lounging next to a badger sow and her cubs. I could go on and on but despite evidence to the contrary you will always have those individuals who will only believe what they want to believe regardless of.

In my past life as a head ranger and wildlife officer my job, particularly when wearing my wildlife officer's hat, tended to create a fair amount of media attention including television. Obviously, I fully expected that side of my life to be over and done with upon retirement but, like many things since I hung up my ranger/wildlife officer boots, my past life has a habit of resurfacing. Whether it be working alongside the police confronting badger diggers and baiters or conservation, both of which still dominate my life to a great degree but what I didn't reckon on was more media coverage particularly with regards to television.

Of course, I had been involved in some television work with regards to the BBC Wales Investigates programme 'The Secret World of Badger Baiters' but that was in a completely different context and didn't directly include me on camera. The limit of my involvement in the media these days merely consisted of the occasional request to write an article for some conservation journal or other, or every once in a while, to perhaps feature in something and as far as I was concerned that was going to be my lot. But once again you never quite know what's around the corner!

In 2019 I was approached by ITV Wales with a view to filming for an episode of their programme 'Coast and Country' which finally resulted in me spending a few days being followed around by a film crew and the presenter as I wandered around the countryside checking my trail cameras, plus being interviewed about my work with the police and RSPCA Special Ops Unit.

During my time I have been followed around by a film crew on many occasions plus filming in a TV studio, but things had moved on a pace since those far off days. Then there were no such things as drones but now I found myself stood in a river going through the motions of checking one of my otter cams explaining to the presenter what I was doing and why, with a cameraman filming on the opposite bank. Then I had to do it all again from another angle but this time merely going through the motions of talking to the presenter who was now sat on the far bank whilst the cameraman piloted a drone to film everything.

Trying to concentrate on the task at hand as a drone buzzes around a few inches above your head like a demented wasp can be a little disconcerting to say the least and takes a little willpower to resist the urge to instinctively swat it out of the sky! Much to the delight of the presenter, who had a passion for old Land Rovers, I had turned up to the location in 'BJ' my 1950 Series 1 Land Rover, and on seeing her, the producer decided that it would be great to include her in the film as it would add another feature to the story, rather than me just strolling around the fields and river bank checking my badger and otter trail cameras whilst nattering to the presenter.

This resulted in them fitting a small camera in BJ's cab to film me in the driver's seat whilst a drone flew high up above filming BJ trundling down the track. I think it took two or three takes before they were happy, but we got there in the end. When it was finally televised in November, there was I merrily driving off down the track in BJ, with clips alternating from me in the driver's seat to others filmed by the drone high above, showing this little old Landy trundling merrily along by the river surrounded by beautiful countryside. A narrative by the presenter accompanied by soothing tranquil music playing in the background added to the scene.

My next foray into the world of television came in March 22 when I was approached by a producer from Athena Films who explained that they had been commissioned by Channel 5 to film a two part program of one hour per episode called 'Badgers: Their Secret World' to be presented by Steve Backshall MBE the naturalist, TV presenter, writer and explorer. She went on to say that this would be the second in the series with the first being 'Fantastic Foxes: Their Secret World' also presented by Steve Backshall and, if I was agreeable, they would like to include some of my trail cam footage of the Nutter clan. After delving further into the proposed general content of the program and watching the first in the series about foxes which, by the way, was extremely well done and educational, I agreed.

Eventually the program began to take shape and I had sent off various snippets of footage to be considered for inclusion, when it was suggested that I should take an active part. The idea was that I would be interviewed, followed by being filmed setting up a trail camera on the drive, to finally sitting on a bench with a few of the No-Tail clan around happily munching away on a few peanuts close by.

I explained that in theory it was a nice idea, but I certainly couldn't guarantee that the badgers would play along as they were only accustomed to mine and my wife Ann's scent. If they suspected something out of the ordinary, they would be off like the clappers back into the wood never to be seen again, at least not that night!

Anyway, the day came for filming and thankfully the weather couldn't have been better. It was fine and bright with hardly a wisp of a breeze. They began with me sat in a chair in the garden being interviewed by the producer. I was asked about the history of the Nutter clan and why they were so christened, plus my views on the garbage banded around regarding badgers predating on sheep and lambs.

I think my reply to that was, 'It's nothing but a load of old codswallop!' followed by stating in no uncertain terms that badgers do not pause a danger in any shape or form to sheep and lambs and I've got ten years of badger sheep interaction video footage to prove it.

With the interview done and dusted my next task was to be filmed setting up a trail camera with Moggy the cat close to my heels making sure that she also got her five minutes of fame. Finally, the time came to set everything up before dusk crept in ready for filming the badgers coming from the wood, through the open gate and onto the drive. Actually, it worked out quite well in respect that the cameraman and Jude the producer tucked themselves away in the half open front porch allowing a good view without being too obvious. With everything in place and darkness beginning to creep in I switched on the security lights to illuminate the scene. The badgers were accustomed to the area being illuminated and were totally unperturbed by the light which of course had the added bonus of making the process of filming that much easier. After scattering a few peanuts around and advising the cameraman and producer to be as silent as possible, with no sniffing, sneezing, scratching of noses or clunking of equipment, I sat myself down on the bench and Moggy, who obviously wanted to raise the odds of her actually being on telly, jumped up to join me.

We didn't have long to wait before the distinctive striped faces of two badgers came sauntering up to the open gate. They paused to sniff the air before backing off a little, they sniffed again and came a little closer, pausing at every other step to raise their heads to take in the smells of the night. They looked directly at me, and then towards the porch and despite the night being still and quiet they were uneasy. They were fully aware of my presence and totally at ease with my scent to the extent that under normal circumstances they would pass under the bench and snuffle around my feet in search of a stray peanut or two. But they sensed that tonight was different. A badger's sense of smell is pretty phenomenal being around 800 times more sensitive than ours and they must have been picking up a plethora of new smells emitted from the two shadowy figures hiding in the porch. But thankfully they didn't let me down and although certainly not as bold as usual the cameraman got the footage in the bag.

A few weeks previous to this, I had set a camera up on a very low tripod on the drive to capture video footage of myself and Moggy sat on the bench whilst a member of the No-Tail clan mooched around looking for peanuts. On this occasion they were indeed passing under the bench and snuffling around my feet and as this was going to be included in the program it took a little of the pressure off with regards to the success of the porch filming.

Filming for television is extremely time consuming and more often than not, hours upon hours of footage will have been edited down to a few minutes when televised. This of course means that when you finally get notified of when it will be on you really have no idea as to what may or may not have been used. In a nutshell your five minutes of fame could have been reduced down to thirty seconds! That's television for you!!

Finally, the filming was completed and loads of my trail cam footage were now at the mercy of the editors. Obviously when making a programme such as this a number of individuals scattered around the UK can be in involved resulting in a tremendous amount of footage having been filmed, and as I said before, you have no idea as to how much you will actually feature in the finished product. As time rolled by periodically the producer would email everyone who took part to say sorry, but Channel 5 haven't given a viewing date as yet, will keep you informed.

Then we were notified that the program was to be televised in Australia on July 23rd but still no date for the UK.

At long last, we were informed that it was going out in the UK at 7pm on 27th and 28th of September 2023. Dates went in diaries, plus the social media coverage, and of course it was advertised by Channel 5 themselves, but to ensure we didn't miss it, videos were set just in case!

Needless to say, Ann and I were glued to the telly for episode one and I was a little surprised to see that within a few minutes they had included a short clip of the Nutter clan charging around like a bunch of idiots one summers evening, plus a few seconds of my ugly mug. It quickly became obvious that like the first in the series featuring foxes, 'Badgers: Their Secret World' was very well done covering a wide range of badger related topics. It was factual and didn't pull any punches! The hour long episode flew by leaving us wanting more and the following night with jobs done and coffee brewed we tuned in to episode two, rather than my thirty seconds or indeed even five minutes of fame I was given much more time, with me popping up throughout the episode. They also included far more of my trail camera footage than I expected including the Nutter clan living up to their name. There was badger and sheep interaction, with sheep and badgers just chilling out together. A couple of clips showed a tiny badger cub wobbling up to a recumbent ewe to touch noses, with another clip showing a totally content ewe just chilling out whilst a cub climbed onto her back. Another showed two of the Nutter clan racing across the large fallen branch forming a natural bridge across the river, with one falling off to go for a swim. Luckily, badgers are very good swimmers!

They showed the otter leaping out of the water to nip the badgers bum plus much, much more, including the footage of me and Moggy on the bench with badgers by my feet and of her tagging on behind as I set up a trail camera on the drive.

She got her wish! The feedback after the viewing was excellent with everyone who cares about, involved in, or previously knew nothing about the species prior to watching it saying how informative it was and that it dispelled quite a few myths along the way.

As mentioned in the program, the only badger the majority of people see are dead ones by the roadside and yet they are numerous as a species but due to their shy, retiring nature and being predominately nocturnal, very few people actually get to see a live wild badger. I'm so lucky in the respect that a great majority of my life has revolved around badgers. Ann and I have hand reared orphaned badger cubs, we have bottle fed them, nurtured them, and ultimately rehabilitated them back to the wild. During the rehabilitation process we have spent months in the woods monitoring them to ensure that their gradual return to the wild goes smoothly. I have confronted badger diggers, been threatened by badger diggers, and given expert evidence in their prosecution.

Time flies by far too quickly and I sometimes find it difficult to comprehend that just over 14 years have passed since I sat in that dingy office of Roger the Codger in Wirral Council's Westminster House HQ as he posed the ridiculous question, 'what are we going to do about these foxes?' referring to Muffles and Velvet my tame, rescued foxes that had lived with me for many years. To refresh your memory, he was posing the question due to the fact that my Wildlife Officer post had gone with me having been, in inverted commas, promoted with my sole duties now consisting of over-seeing the management of a large ranger service. Which, according to Roger the Codger, did not include caring for two wayward foxes! Anyway, as you will have read in the first chapter. I won that one!

Two years later I jumped at the offer of early retirement, and we relocated to sunny North Wales, and once again if my writings have interested you enough to get to this stage of the book, you will be familiar with my journey over the past 12 years. I have put pen to paper and wrote my story, From Badgers to Nighthawks' published in 2019, followed by 'The Tales of Old Billy Badger' and now 'From Otters to Badger Baiters,' The sequel to 'From Badgers to Nighthawks'.

But what next?

Well, since first writing this chapter, 2024 has been busy!

March is drawing to a close and already I have given evidence on two occasions with possibly two more cases awaiting court dates. I know for a fact that I will get a call from the police at some point in the very near future resulting in yet another ride in a police car to investigate yet more badger related crime which will no doubt generate another brow beating by a defence lawyer.

My publisher – Beul Aithris Publishing has already mooted the idea of another book, this time solely on badgers and possibly titled *Badgers, Fact, Myth and Fiction* and in April I'm scheduled for a spot of filming for BBC 2's Springwatch!

Any finally, the sun is setting, the badgers are awakening and it's almost time to scatter a few peanut treats.

And with that I will bid you farewell.

www.ingramcontent.com/pod-product-compliance
Lightning Source LLC
Chambersburg PA
CBHW030010290326
41934CB00005B/288